Praise for Regarding Willingness

"Tom Harpole is what you might call a thinking man's Evel Knievel. Not many folks can so casually catalogue a long list of traumas they've heaped upon themselves and still maintain the glint in their eye. Harpole has logged a lot of crazy and interesting stories in the journal of his life." — Aaron Parrett, author of *Montana: Then and Now*

"Harpole loves to diffuse danger with humor and doesn't avoid sardonic comments about certain world affairs. ... (This book) is a testament to his willingness to take on any endeavor—the riskier the better—to live the experience and get the story." — Montana Quarterly

"When Tom Harpole talks of his story assignments and adventures, there's a sense that this guy just may be channeling the energy and spirit of Jack London and Mark Twain with a dash of George Plimpton." — *Independent Record*

"Harpole's rambunctious and affectionate yarns recall Montana's powerful and often hilarious folktale tradition. At the same time, he has elevated the art of risk-taking to a form of spiritual practice. This wonderful book—filled with thrills, chills, and rough-and-ready humor—deserves to find many devoted readers." — Rick Newby, editor of *The New Montana Story: An Anthology*

"Whether he's free-falling over the Ukraine with a band of Cosmonaut skydivers, riding shotgun on winter passage up the world's most treacherous ice road, or just kicking back to explain the nuances of high angle Mach 2 pasture sledding, the sheer breadth of experience Harpole explores in this collection is enough to take your breath away. The fact he's also a first-class writer sets these essays light years apart from the norm." — Fred Haefele, author of *Rebuilding the Indian*

"Harpole has a fearless sense of adventure, and his exploits take the reader into experiences many would like to have but would not attempt. Life lived to the fullest emanates from his pages with humor and danger, adventure and adrenaline told with literary skill. The adage that fact is stranger than fiction shows its wisdom in his essays. With these stories of life, told with a sharp eye and a keen ear, Tom has given us an extraordinary piece of Americana." — Scott G. Hibbard, author of *Beyond the Rio Gila* (spring 2021)

Other titles from Riverfeet Press

THIS SIDE OF A WILDERNESS: A Novel (2013) - Daniel J. Rice

THE UNPEOPLED SEASON: Journal from a North Country Wilderness (2014) - Daniel J. Rice

WITHIN THESE WOODS: A collection of Northwoods nature essays with original illustrations by the author (2015) - Timothy Goodwin

ECOLOGICAL IDENTITY: Finding Your Place in a Biological World (2016) - Timothy Goodwin

TEACHERS IN THE FOREST: Essays from the last wilderness in Mississippi Headwaters country (2016) - Barry Babcock

ROAD TO PONEMAH: The Teachings of Larry Stillday (2016) - Michael Meuers

A FIELD GUIDE TO LOSING YOUR FRIENDS (2017) - Tyler Dunning

AWAKE IN THE WORLD (2017): a collection of stories, poems, and essays about wildlife, adventure, and the environment

ONE-SENTENCE JOURNAL (winner of the 2018 Montana Book Award and the 2019 High Plains Book Award) - Chris La Tray

WILDLAND WILDFIRES: and where the wildlife go (2018) - Randie Adams

I SEE MANY THINGS: Ninisidawenemaag, Book I (2019) - Erika Bailey-Johnson

AWAKE IN THE WORLD, V.II (2019): a collection of stories, poems, and essays about wildlife, adventure, and the environment

FAMILIAR WATERS (2020) - David Stuver

BURNT TREE FORK: A Novel (2020) - J.C. Bonnell

LIFE LIST: Poems (2020) - Marc Beaudin

KAYAK CATE (2021) - Cate Belleveau

Regarding Willingness

Tom Harpole

Livingston, MT

Riverfeet Press
Livingston, MT 59047
www.riverfeetpress.com

REGARDING WILLINGNESS

Chronicles of a Fraught Life

Tom Harpole

Edited by Daniel J. Rice

ISBN-13: 978-1-7360894-0-8

LCCN: 2020949469

10 9 8 7

This title is available at a special discount to booksellers and libraries. Send inquiries to: riverfeetpress@gmail.com

Cover design by Jonathan Millman

Cover photo by Lisa Ernst

Mayfly illustration by Timothy Goodwin

Typesetting & interior design by Daniel J. Rice

Riverfeet Press is proud to be Made in Montana.

I worked on shining and amending these essays, on and off, while watching, wondering at, and loving my granddaughter as she grew into her sixth year. She inspires me.

I dedicate this tome to:
Payton Riley Herbert

CONTENTS

Foreword

This book project began, as I suppose do most things, with a seemingly small and inconsequential event. I had posted a photo on Facebook of a man throwing coffee from his cup into the freezing winter air. One could see from the picture that the coffee was falling to the ground as ice. The next day there was a comment from a Tom Harpole saying that he had done that once. I asked him how cold it had to be for this to occur. He answered that he'd written about it and would email the story. Thus I read the first of many of Tom's splendid tales, "A Matter of Degrees." We corresponded over the next few months as he continued to send me more of his writings and I became hooked. His writings were well crafted and flowed easily. The stories were amazing tales of deeds that very few of us would willingly attempt. As the stories continued to arrive, I found myself traveling with Tom in an eighteen-wheeler over the Alaskan ice road at eighty below; to Russia to skydive with Russian cosmonauts; of breaking his thumb while setting an NFL record; of getting a bear stoned; of free-falling from 12,000 feet with a peregrine falcon; and of flying over Montana in a homemade aircraft.

Out of his writings, Tom emerged as a bright and sincere human who always said yes to the opportunities presented in doing new and extraordinary things. A man whose willingness to experience life thrust him deeply into the world (Tom had logged some 1.5 million air miles traveling the globe in search of stories). I sent his writings on to friends and soon discovered that it wasn't just me who really loved Tom's writing. That is when the idea of getting these stories together in a book occurred to me. They had all been published over the years in various national magazines, and the thought of them languishing unread in dusty archives didn't seem right. The stories deserved to be made available to the reading public for the many hours of pleasurable reading they would bring. I brought up the idea with Tom and at first he seemed unsure if this would be feasible. I think that we humans see ourselves and our accomplishments less clearly than others sometimes do. It seemed to me that Tom believed his writings of three decades ago had lost their relevance. I was determined to convince him otherwise. After months of corresponding with Tom, he and I finally met face to face. We talked of this and that for a bit and then I broached the subject of an anthology. I guess that my enthusiasm won him over. When we parted company that day, he was almost as excited as I was.

We then did some networking among friends in search of a publisher. Andrea Peacock, of Elk River Books in Livingston, MT, gave me the email address for Daniel Rice of Riverfeet Press. I contacted him and explained that I was helping a friend and had samples of his writings which I hoped would interest him as a publisher. He asked me to email the writings and I suggested instead that I present them in person. I was certain that my enthusiasm would load the scales in Tom's favor. Daniel did indeed like what he read, and within three weeks Tom and he signed a contract on the banks of the Yellowstone River. I attended the ceremony as the very pleased midwife.

I would like to make one suggestion to the reader; that you read these stories as I first did: Read each story with a space of time between them. I know that your impulse will be to devour the book in one gulp, but the tales told here are so unique that each deserves a bit of time for thought and reflection. Hang on and enjoy the journey!

— Loren Haarr
Harlowton, MT
Sept. 2020

Regarding Willingness

Tom Harpole

Members of the Harpole family, circa 1956. Tom front and center.

Disarming and Decimating Myself

Author note: This essay, written in my late sixties, is an attempt to make sense of a multitude of traumatic turns in my life. A fraught life may be full or dangerous, it depends on one's attitude.

In my ninth year on this planet, my dad, Phil Harpole, door-to-door bible salesman, on Easter Sunday, photographed his seven extant kids and his wife, Mary, who was pregnant with our penultimate sibling, John. Philip followed about fourteen months after John. Our block on St. Paul Street harbored as many as sixty kids on any given day, nine of whom my mom, Mary Elizabeth Harpole, added to the mostly Irish Catholic neighborhood. Two families on our street had back-yard trampolines. A parental permission slip to jump on their tramp was required by the family with twelve kids whose accountant dad was never seen except between his company car and front door. The no-rules trampoline owner, two houses down the elm-bowered old street, who never asked us kids for parental permission, was a Protestant high school math teacher with one kid and no wife and he unwittingly host-ed a kind of *Lord of the Flies* mild west wilderness area comprising preteen boys cultivating precancerous habits and incipient bubbahood.

In my early days, there on St. Paul street, I grew up in a devout Roman Catholic family that would not eat meat on a Friday, would never miss confession on Saturday or Mass on Sunday, and who were not allowed to set foot in another faith's church, even for a wedding. It was a sin for women to enter a Catholic church without covering their head; birth control was forbidden, and no woman was allowed on the altar. Using certain cuss words was regarded as a mortal sin, another on a long list of transgressions, including masturbating, that were to be punished by eternity in Hell, according to every nun who taught in Catholic schools. I might as well interject here that when my Dad died unexpectedly in 1966, at age 46, and left my Mom with nine kids under 18 to raise, the nun who summoned me over the intercom—out of history class and into her office—this black clad stout minion of the Church sat behind her desk and said, "Mr. Harpole, you're going to have to show more character than you've been exhibiting. Your father died about an hour ago at Mercy hospital." And there went my faith in Catholicism and my belief in its flunkies. My karma ran over my dogma, so to speak. The safety net of God's love got pulled and as I walked two miles home, I understood that the holiness I aspired to was as warped and worthless as that nun. Mom, my siblings, and I had to exercise much willingness for the relatively tough life ahead, and at the time I learned that accepting risks in the face of eternal damnation might work out as the rule makers exposed themselves as dishonest and confused. And then the Church rescinded the age-old injunctions against the sins they'd insisted were the ultimate transgressions, imparting to me that existential consequences that are imposed and promoted by other humans are there to be disregarded, and that I could proceed with accepting risks.

The great blessing of my early years is that I wound up with eight siblings. It seemed as though Mom was perpetually looking after two or three diapered toddlers, and hadn't the time to be involved with her preteen offspring's neighborhood doings. We were expected to show up in her kitchen at 10 in the morning to wash a vitamin down with a glass of juice and a have a cookie, but from about the age of ten I eschewed the healthy treat and was usually to be found with my friends, the trampoline delinquents, over in the Keller's back yard, smoking purloined Pall Malls and filtered Viceroys, laughing hoarsely, and bouncing. We figured out how to make each other faint, jumped onto, and back off the steep garage roof, and experimented with fist-fighting. Several of us had been instructed on the proprieties and fine points of bare knuckle fist-fighting by WWII veteran dads and uncles who fought in Korea in the early fifties. You never hit a guy wearing glasses. If a guy wore a ring, he'd remove it. We always looked the other guy in the eye and shook hands afterward. I made a few friends observing such rituals. We practiced high degree-of-difficulty trampoline tricks with nosebleeds occasionally trailing scarlet arcs against true blue skies. We were novices in the school of feckless abandon.

Give an attentive ten year old no-joke boxing lessons and you have a kid who will always, "Dish out more than they took, and they'll take on anybody," the mindset of our bellicose, but heedful elders. We propounded: "Never start a fight, but finish it." In our proscribed parochial parish, tolerating pain in the pursuit of fun and justice was *de rigueur*. Laughing off injuries conferred a certain status. My willingness to risk dire consequences for attempts at exciting, albeit somewhat nuts activities, started at a young age and ratcheted up from there.

Occasionally, some bigger guys who didn't fit in to our tribe would show up and annoy the hell out of us, flaunting their status as teenagers and ignoring our rules. They'd swagger into the Keller's backyard acting like they belonged there and we cut them slack, but us guys watched for some infraction of the tacit laws of *trampolinedom*. The one rule every trampoline jumper must respect was that you absolutely never, no excuses, bounced with your shoes on. Who wore shoes in the summer anyway? Should the interlopers push their luck, jumping with their high topped Converse Chucks tied tight, or just act a little snotty, the fight was on and although they were mostly bigger than us, none of them really understood how to throw a punch. Our vigilantism was just asking for swelling, cut lips, and bruising inflicted by teenaged guys, but our territoriality usually prevailed. Early on I inured myself to all but the most dramatic injuries and pain. In the midst of my eight siblings, I easily concealed shiners and scuffed knuckles, which no one cared to acknowledge anyway.

Most summers I'd break a bone while jumping and be sidelined for a few weeks. Since those heady days of bouncing in the sixties, I've not gone twelve months without an E.R. visit. The quick leg-up to zero gravity that trampolines bestow—that split second of adrenaline fizz at the top of the ascent—still seduces me. Despite all the broken bones and scar tissue measured in feet, I keep showing up for more pursuits that end up planting me on the sidelines. Perhaps I should feel benighted or unworthy about those days and weeks of trauma, but plain, honest curiosity, and the pursuit of survivor's euphoria have propelled me through life and given me to admire our species' need to challenge gravity and common sense. My heedless heart for attempting meaningless feats, I guess, derives from my belief that if somebody else has done it, and it attracts me, maybe I'll figure it out.

Curiosity and a certain hankering after new ways to have fun, and getting paid to write about pursuits that require hardhats or helmets, has provided me with a lot of writing material for decades. My efforts to write about certain oddball fixes for my adventure joneses have provided me with dozens of published essays and feature articles for glossy national magazines in which I report on outlandish human avocations that generally call for skull protection. There are some excellent helmets around anymore, and reasons to don them abound. We boomers grew up deriding helmets with phrases like, "skid lids" and "brain buckets." I showed up too early for today's value-your-skull culture that began providing bespoke helmets for any activity. Not that I always get the short end of the stick. Occasionally, I accidentally prevail even when the odds weren't conducive. But when I have come up short and got messed up boxing, logging, bull riding, sledding, skiing, skydiving, paragliding, and climbing trees with a chainsaw, I strive to just get on with my life. As Henry Stamper said, in Ken Kesey's, "Sometimes a Great Notion," "When you fall, fall, in the direction of your work." I've learned to accept the trauma and adapt to temporary disabilities and compensate for the long-term losses.

A couple of years ago I ran a chainsaw through my left arm while I was about 35 feet up a dead standing ponderosa pine. I'd intended to take the hazardous old thing down on the campus of Carroll College in Helena where I played freshman basketball until I fractured my skull in 1968. I covered the core curriculum there and sang in the choir until 1970 when mounting school loans and the draft lottery short stopped my formal education. Long story. For a couple decades, horse logging, timber falling and working with high explosives were all I seemed to need, until the early '80s, when I so seriously damaged my body logging that I turned to writing for a living. After 22 years of writing features that usually required foreign travel, I'd racked up

1.5 million miles on Delta flights, I was burned out at about the same time the magazines I'd been gratefully working for put a lid on travel expenses, so I'd been back doing the arborist deal for a few years, and my son-in-law, Andy Herbert was becoming one of the best hands at tree work I'd ever been around.

I was up that big pine on my alma mater because I had to remove two thick limbs that could have damaged the landscaping where I intended to lay the old hooter down. Mostly, what I was thinking about was persuading this tall, limby pine on the ground in the direction where it wasn't leaning. Concurrent with that need was the fact that if I didn't tip it over strategically, it would still require two semi loads to haul away the trunk and massive limbs which Andy and I would have to drag an extra hundred feet or so. I'd often disregarded basic safety rules when I worked alone and never answered to anyone, until Andy began working with me. The pine was roughly 36 inches in diameter, too big to climb with my tree spurs and flip line, so I climbed my sketchy old 28 foot extension ladder without harnessing up. We'd set the tall ladder up on the south side of the tree because the bull pine was leaning to the north. I was hustling up into this tree's mid-section because a propitious wind had been gusting out of the northwest that would help me tip the tree to the southeast where I intended to make it fall as soon as I could get back on the ground and could make the chainsaw cuts and pound wedges into those saw kerfs that would cause it to fall where I wanted it to, avoiding damaging the landscaping around its stout, belled-out base. I needed to quickly saw two limbs off before the helpful morning winds died down or shifted. One limb was intact, about 13 feet long and four inches in diameter where it grew from the bole of the tree. Above it, partially separated from the bole, hanging vertically and swinging in the gusts, was the second limb I had to remove, and then there was a third limb, my left arm, that my chainsaw found that last time I climbed a tree.

Sometimes loggers and arborists rush the work and get mangled simply because they're under pressure to save time, taking shortcuts that are ill advised. Here, I intended to avoid damaging the meticulously groomed campus landscaping, and if I did this right, it would save several hours of drudgery, dragging about five tons of limbs and trunk to our dumpster truck's access area. I started my chainsaw up there and grabbed the intact limb at about my ribcage level with my left hand so I could huck it out beyond the drip edge of the tree. I revved my "top saw," a specially designed tree climber's saw that may be deployed one-handed while the arborist is climbing around in treetops. I intended to sever the horizontal limb when a sudden gust slammed the upper vertically swinging limb into my right arm, which held the full throttle saw. That swinging limb slapped my right elbow hard enough that for a split second I had no control of the saw and it buried itself in my left forearm, a couple inches below my elbow. I thought, "Everything has just changed." In less than a second I lost the use of my arm, which was barely attached and laying atop the limb I'd meant to saw off. They resembled each other proportionally, but my limb was awash in pulsing, welling, vivid red blood. My arm more closely resembled the swinging tree limb that had just driven the chainsaw through it; it was hanging on by some stubborn strands of connective tissue, muscle, and the remains of the ulnar bone. With just the tops of the cutters visible, the three inch wide bar and chain were buried in my arm in a kerf that angled towards my elbow. I lifted the saw out of my arm and two severed arteries pumped blood into the air above me and the tree trunk and ladder below me, cascading onto Andy. He got showered with my blood, but kept steadying the ladder. I heard him call 911 and he told me he was removing his belt for a tourniquet.

A fully wound up top saw moves the chain around the bar at 88 feet per second, or 55 mph. Meat and bone do not impede a Stihl top saw one bit. My memory of the ensuing events and vignettes are a little fuzzy, bear with me here. I felt hopeful, for a couple breaths. A quick sort of fantasy briefly bemused me that this wasn't that serious, that I'd just get patched up somehow, but the blood spraying and spurting all around disabused me of my denial mechanism. My blood coated nearby surfaces and fell away from me to the manicured lawn where Andy, our work truck, and our arborist equipment were strewn around the hillside landscape down there. This incomprehensible dilemma occurred to me piecemeal, over a couple more breaths that bought me time to understand that this was real and I had very little time to react.

During my ten years as a volunteer EMT I attended 32 hours per year of continuing education and somewhere along the way I learned that humans can exsanguinate in less than two minutes with two arteries pumping plasma. My blood was arcing from my arm about eight feet, which was the most dramatic thing I've seen my body do since the trampoline days. I found that I could reach into my pulpy forearm, avoiding the raw, cut bone ends and I could squash down or pinch off the arteries. I didn't entertain any notion that I'd just wait up there for help. I had to get back down on the ground as quickly as I could. Andy, of course, had seen the bloody top saw drop, and despite the bloody showering he was enduring, he quietly encouraged me to get myself down. Uncertainty about the present and future of my left arm was a terrible subtext. My muscle memory from thousands of tree descents seemed to count for nothing, I was moving awkwardly, I had blood on my glasses and I was unsure of where my feet were going. Limiting blood loss and descending one-armed right now were the only goals I had in mind. I paused in my descent a few times and groped into the gaping maw, and pinched and squashed off the blood flow, and I meant to compose myself, then I'd grasp the tacky ladder as the scarlet squirts resumed. Pause, probe, squash, pinch, descend three or four rungs, repeat; I thought it went okay but my vision was fading as I grew light-headed. Numerous folks have asked if it hurt. Humans can't exactly recall pain. We know that a sensory overload was the central theme of our existence for a while but we cannot recall how any given injury actually felt. That's why women may have more than one baby. That's why fools like me must resort to euphemism and denial about the very real pain that I've so often visited upon myself. Human bodies are always evolving, and there's never been a reward for acknowledging pain. We evolved understanding that announcing or in any way vocalizing about injuries just brought the predators on.

I had my right shoulder, elbow and wrist busted and crushed by a falling tree that kept me down overnight in the early 80's, the after effects chase me around decades later. After way too many Montana Band-Aids, bought by Worker's Comp, they allowed me to head to the Johns Hopkins hospital, a vaunted but shabby collection of buildings in a murderous Baltimore neighborhood where I underwent nine surgeries in two years. To allay pain, they prescribed more than 3,500 OxyContin in about three years. The opioids helped, but they're sickening and cause constipation and depression and exacerbate the complete self-absorption where chronic pain was incrementally taking me. I crawled under the self-centered rock of depression until my kids admitted that the medicated version of the old man was scaring them. It wasn't much of a leap for a pantheist to go veterinary. My first real job was cleaning up dog shit and observing dogs at a veterinary hospital in Denver in 1963. I now aspire to emulate the pain response dogs elicit. They have it dialed in. Dogs don't appear to acknowledge chronic problems. They compensate. Play, sexual curiosity, and food distract them as the healing proceeds. This course is worth cultivating. Buy time. By and by, pain will cut you some slack.

Up in that tree, I felt no pain. I understood the fact that I could die this day, but the task at hand kept my thoughts focused. I wasn't thinking much past getting myself down and Andy applying a tourniquet. I sensed my brain function declining, but, at 66, that's a familiar misgiving. Numerous folks have offered the opinion that I was too old to still be climbing trees. I'd heard such admonitions for a few years. I considered and dismissed them as merely self-referencing. For twenty years my chosen vocation—climbing and tipping tricky trees, paid well enough to buy me time for reading and writing. For about 22 years, magazine writing paid the bills even as accumulated logging injuries had their way with me. My final act of denial may well be feigning indignity for living long enough to experience the decrepitude that I have inflicted upon my body for as long as I can remember. But I asked for it.

A gal I dated for a couple years, who was the smartest of all, and generally used her smarts for funny, believes that there are no accidents, that humans somehow call down misfortune upon themselves. I couldn't argue with her, given my crash dummy track record, but I couldn't reconcile her beliefs with, say, an infant being assaulted. A grizzly jumped her one morning, while she walked her dog along the upper Yellowstone river, and by that evening she regarded the attack as the most spiritual experience of her life. I hope she sticks with her story. Consistent spirituality adds up.

Pushing a chainsaw running full bore through my left arm was not at all spiritual at first blush, it was a totally losing deal with no concurrent epiphanies or apparent silver linings. I regarded the gory mess where the chainsaw bar had been buried in my arm and the cartoonishly squirting arteries and I realized that blood is terrifically fascinating in ways you don't usually see. It blanketed the ponderosa bark. It flowed lavishly but languidly, coagulating like cooling lava down the sun-bleached pinkish extension ladder. I was peripherally aware that I might not be alive in a couple minutes, but thoughts of diminished longevity in no way chased me down that ladder. Besides, I figure that longevity is a matter of plain, dumb luck. My cousin Gus, a reluctantly retired doctor, reasoned with me when my prostate blood test spiked, and the urologist wanted to do a biopsy. Googling had turned up the phrase, "Death Sentence." I called Gus, and he said, "Get off fookin' Google," he's always been one for euphony. "Prostate cancer's slow. Don't let them do the biopsy. Forget about the PSA numbers game, there's false positives," he said. Then briefly abandoning his bedside manner, he added, "The way you've been going, my moneys on something else getting you first anyway." I trust Gus, he does not traffic in platitudes.

Before something else gets me, I wanted to write about sawing through my arm. I did my research. On the unassailable internet I Googled "auto amputation," and perused cases of people who have cut off their own limb/s or hired it done. Many, on the progression of websites that appeared, did so because they were sexually aroused by the idea of being an amputee (apotemnophilia). There are also those who have cut off their own limbs because they believe the limb doesn't belong to them, i.e., Body Integrity Identity Disorder, a.k.a. Amputee Identity Disorder or xenomelia. I do not dismiss those mindsets. But the sordid depths one might explore when the body endures such a transformation are beyond my ken, beyond imagining. Some internet auto-amputation stories are of those who have self-amputated to survive, as did Aron Ralston, the plucky canyoneer who, after 127 hours with his arm pinned by a rock, finally committed to cutting it off with a pocket knife. Human behavior is endlessly interesting, especially so when we face an uncertain, but permanent change we have not chosen.

Sometimes, however, some guys, (always guys), seem to volunteer for such changes. I'm entertained by guys –always guys – who say, "I'd cut my left arm off for…" or "I'd give a leg for…" or "I'd give my left nut for…" The object of this morbid sacrifice is usually a vehicle (to be sure, it should be equipped with an automatic transmission), or an otherwise unattainable sexual experience in which safety may not even be an afterthought. Honestly, have you ever heard a woman wish to self-mutilate in exchange for quickie sex or a cool car?

My first detached reflection as a fresh "amputee," on terra firma was that I was bereft and my life had changed ineluctably right there up a bull pine on my old campus. I majored in English, where they tacitly discouraged single syllable usage. Okay, in that moment I didn't think "bereft," or "ineluctably," but I intuited that my life had just changed beyond imagining. In a language lover's effort to eschew cliché I dismissed self-pity, which could preempt redemption; reducing this event to the quotidian. I avoided uttering dirty words, even gateway curses like "son of a gun." Cussing these days has become crass, pedestrian; diminished through heedless repetition in both drama and evocation. My heart was wantonly pumping my blood all over the place while my vision narrowed as if I were squinting through gauze. With Andy's help I slumped upon a low stone retaining wall, one of the features I had not wanted to damage with the weight of the old pine crashing down.

Andy dredged up his ski-patroller's first responder training. But he was an amputation virgin; one just doesn't encounter such visceral stuff when patrolling ski hills. He minded my immediate, most vital needs. He applied his belt tourniquet to the point that he didn't think he could hold it much longer, as he kept saving my life. The ambulance arrived and delivered me with siren, lights, and alacrity to the Helena hospital where they administered a few units of second hand blood during which time a kind nurse offhandedly brushed bloody wood chips off my pants, which made me reckon there was hope for me. I was packaged for a helicopter ride to Great Falls because the lower portion of my arm, which wasn't getting any blood, would die if we attempted the 90 minute drive. Before they loaded me in the helicopter, a male nurse with furry forearms I envied, inflated three pneumatic tourniquets on my arm. I do recall the pain of those things squeezing my upper arm shut to be significant. As I was rolled out to the helipad a doctor who didn't introduce herself said she could give me a shot that could help with the pain if I could focus on something pleasant. In the turbine racket of the helo she rather daintily asked me if I'd ever experimented with psychotropic drugs. "They never proved anything," I said, and tried to smile. She shrugged wryly, said, "Think good thoughts, sir," and shot me up on the helipad.

As they loaded me and secured the gurney, I focused on a dear friend with whom I have played music for about 30 years, the sweetest, kindest, calmest woman in Montana. Those pleasantries carried me gracefully on the 21 minute, $33,000 ride to Great Falls, during which I also slipped into a reverie about what comprises dismemberment. Entertaining such thoughts elevated on an unknown drug, at 8,000 feet, made sense, because the three-person, helmeted and headsetted crew never said a word to me. The good docs in Helena had imparted the message that they only ordered a helicopter because they didn't have all the specialists it would take to reattach my arm. I spent four days in the Great Falls hospital while self-administering all the morphine I could stand. My kids showed up and hauled me home, a ride for which I have no certain memories.

My son, Derry, moved up from Bozeman to work with Andy and the tree business loped along without me. Over the next few months a verdant spring yielded to summer's swelter, which segued into autumn aromas and by November I could scratch my chin with my left hand again. The top saw I dropped became a for-parts saw, but was befouled with blood. The extension ladder still exhibited blood on the tracks along the sides by fall, when tree work tapered off for the winter.

Three years later there isn't much sensation in that arm. I'm careful about heat sources near my hand, which had been disfigured for quite a few years. I decimated my manicure one evening during a Scrabble game out at the ranch. No one enters a Scrabble game thinking, "Whoa, I could lose a finger doing this." But, of course, I managed to lose half my wedding ring finger in the course of a Scrabble game. (You know how people get). The truth is, someone was taking so long making a play that I went outside to set off a few mortar rounds, those gorgeous fireworks we see exploding and flowering in the night sky on the 4th of July. I'd launched two, then lit one with a short fuse and before I could drop it in the tube the detonator, propellant, and an encompassing, psychedelic green starburst went off in my left hand. When my headlamp cut through the acrid smoke, I saw that my ring finger was now my shortest finger, while my pinkie was stuck pointing perpendicularly, which still lends a certain elegance even when I don't need it, as when drinking wine or running a chainsaw.

As I beheld my stumpy left ring finger I felt that this was rich writing territory. Smoke wisped up from what was left of my cauterized finger. I spit on two matchhead-sized flames, which were illuminating my exposed bone. I knew, then, that the wound would not be very theatrical because it bled very little, which alleviated the trauma and attenuated the drama, suggesting that I could improvise a jocular reaction to this turn of events.

I walked back in the house hoping to marginalize this asinine act. Entertaining the Scrabble players near my picture window had cost me one digit out of ten, thus the word, "decimate." The Scrabblers were intent. I hovered, inspecting the board and asked, "Where we at?" My kids and their pals looked up with warm, somewhat unfocused expressions, but as I drew my unsettling paw from behind my back, the aspects of the gamers changed. We had all been keeping secrets; I had intended to reveal mine incrementally, while distracting them with a bit of badinage. But the playful discourse shut down as chair legs grated away from the kitchen table. The philistines started in with their eye rolling. I blurted, "I can drive," which was met with a chorus of derisive snorts and more of that puerile eye rolling. My daughter, Flannery, drove the 37 miles over the Divide to the Helena hospital. On the way I tried chuckling as a hapless, chastened pyrotechnic dude. I've been a practicing, licensed explosives engineer since 1974. I sheepishly check-listed explosives protocols, I'd just broken a prime directive of handling short fuses, and I was paying with a finger.

Dignity and thoughtfulness in trauma are moods I can affect. As we drove, I strove to teach my adult kids how to handle extreme examples of adversity by my dopey musings on this event. It's gratifying to believe that I can still impart or suggest anything to them these days, especially, in retrospect, while I was in shock. I did not bring them up to tolerate miscreants like me. Raising my kids, it seemed about all I had to remember was to encourage resourcefulness, be nice, and don't reward bullshit. Same with the dozens of highway trauma victims I'd attended to as a volunteer EMT. Extending compassion underlaid and informed my every action at an accident scene, but I've often told traumatized humans to do something for themselves, like raising a wounded extremity above their heart while applying pressure on a dressing. It helps them feel less victimized. That's not jaded, it's compassionate. Right?

The E.R. doctor in Helena had patched me up a few times. He benumbed my ragged little stump and used carpenter's tools to fix it. With a 26,000 rpm Dremel tool he ground down the charred bone.

He made some judicious snips, then sewed the intact flaps of skin to-gether and left me with antibiotics, a pain pill prescription, and a rather stern injunction to not show up again for a while. What ever happened to the solace of job security, or, *the customer is always right?* I was miffed by the disapproving tone he chose. Why can't some people see the lighter side of things?

In dire straits, levity enhances sanity, and is my go-to affectation. But humor is complicated. Blowing a finger off or, say, cutting your own arm off, on the face of it, ain't funny. As an essayist, I seek to uphold my end of a contract with readers and hope to give them my distinct, if odd, slant on topics, while hewing to my versions of truth and proper usage.

I've been trying to write this disarming essay for a few years. The combination of hospital drugs, selective amnesia, and breaking all my ribs about a year later, just before I had to get my right shoulder and some vertebrae fused, followed by a knee replacement last summer, have conspired to keep me too numb to trust my writing. I am, how-ever, back practicing again.

Thank you, dear reader.

The Last of Butch

(previously published by Faber & Faber, London)

Author Note: This autobiographical piece was selected as The Best Short Story of 1986 in the British Isles, and published in an anthology, *First Fictions*, which led to the Irish Arts Council inviting me to return and participate as one of ten writers in the Irish National Writers Workshop, in 1987. I was the first Irish/American dual national to be selected for this national workshop.

The envelope felt spongy. It came from a wet place. The Southeast Alaska Logger's Association was notifying me to make arrangements to collect Butch at the Portland Airport in two weeks: the time and flight number, that was it.

Butch had been falling timber up on some islands in the Tongass forest in Southeast Alaska. He'd started off at Port Alice. My cousin Charlie mentioned he'd run across him at a bar in Ketchikan. He was always the top-dollar faller on any high lead show and word of his presence sort of resonated out. In the nine months since he'd left I got one postcard scrawled in yellow logger's crayon that said: "Harp: Big Wood, Big Money. See Ya In The Sun, Butch."

Butch was an element of the forest. The woods weren't supposed to hand him less than a living. But a fair few loggers I'd known were dead or crippled from this tough life that young men made harder than it had to be. We all regarded the work as a thrill ride that we'd only get a few years to do. Old loggers are usually around 50, and they have been deliberate, careful, and conservative.

I'd heard, perhaps half a dozen times, the seven long toots on high-lead tower whistles echo against mountainsides, a signal to shut down the whole show for the day when someone had been mutilated or killed; sliced in half between a wire rope and a stump when some "anger logger," as Butch called them, heedlessly reeled in a haulback cable too fast, too soon. Some guys just got crumpled into oblivion in the myriad accidents that happen on steep ground when all that cylindrical weight moving under our puny human influence finally cuts loose, bowling and batting and crushing us as we wondered what just happened for a second or two.

None of those mishaps ever gave two weeks notice. I couldn't shake the thought of big bad news coming slowly. The post office lobby closed in around me. I stuffed the letter under my slicker, stepped out into the drizzle, and drove back up into the clouds on Pedee Mountain, where I had my one-man, two-horse logging camp set up.

An airline guy in a red sport coat had Butch in a wheelchair. I looked for casts, splints, or braces as they came up the concourse. Butch grinned and announced, "Hey Harp. Rode first class. Free beverages. That plane lost money on me."

"Butch, can't you walk?" I asked. Both of his legs had boots at the bottom.

"I got on feeling puny, and right now I'd only come up with a piss-poor stagger. Oh, Harp, this here's Eddie. Eddie, my friend Harp," he said, and coughed wetly down at his lap. "Eddie's a good guy."

Eddie smiled, "Butch, may I help you to your friend's car?"

"You may, Eddie. Might as well," Butch said. He accepted the ride in the wheelchair as though he was used to it.

He'd lost a lot of weight. The nape of his neck looked pinched. His head bobbed like an old man's as we wove through the airport. He smiled up at me and shrugged. His curly blond beard was browned around the mouth by the countless cigarettes he'd cantilevered off his lip while his hands were busy.

We emerged into the jet fuel smog and machinery noises outside the airport; the fumes and high decibels were comforting. We'd done a lot of logging and living together in diesel stink and mechanical rackets.

"Butch," I half-shouted, "you look like hell."

"You ought to see it from in here," he croaked. "Thanks for your time, Eddie." He tipped him fifty bucks and climbed into the pickup while I kneed his old backpack into the bed. As the massive, concrete airport and its ramps receded in our wake we made small talk. Butch treated me to a few vignettes about cutting down old growth spruce, seaplane rides to work, and helicopter logging on rain forest islands as we drove through the city traffic, skying over concrete bridges stacked three-high that cambered over the Willamette River. He spoke of working on slopes so steep his lungs burned all day. We headed south-westerly, towards the Coast Range, where Butch had grown up.

Finally:

"Pleurisy, Harp. Then after two weeks in the goddam Ketchikan clinic the doctor said it was lung cancer. Both lungs. Terminal lung cancer ..."

His voice came at me like cyclists coasting by conversing; a rapid ticking rattled me from ear to ear. I wouldn't or couldn't make out what he was saying.

Then:

"Half of all doctors graduate in the lower 50 percent of their class, ya know. Culls all go to Alaska. Doping me and bullshitting them-selves."

I asked him to slow down. He'd always been an alpha, articulate drunk.

"Butch, how you gonna kick it?"

"It's terminal, you know what ..."

"Bullshit, bullshit, no ..."

"Harp, listen — watch the road, goddamnit — the clichés and wet eyes and bibles and bargains are starting for you. I'm done with 'em. They told me a month ago. Indulge yourself. I did. Hell, a guy has to. I came back to die. I want it to be a decent time in my life." He coughed into both hands, studied them, wiped them on his black jeans and said,

"Trust me, you'll get used to it." He flopped his arm across the seat back, squeezed my shoulder and said, "I trust you. Once things settle it'll be okay. I could have a good six months left."

Willamette Valley backroads skirt the valley's river bottom fields as though the farmers had laid them out. Our destination was the background of the movie in the windshield. A clearcut-soothing salve of mist obscured the lower reaches of the Coast Range, leaving the blue timbered peaks bathing in the afternoon sun. Butch slumped back and rested his head over the seat top, but his eyes were eager. He noticed where the Coast Range ridgelines had been altered since he'd left. He looked at watersheds five miles distant; horizons with precipitous edges where missing second growth fir described the boundaries of recent clearcuts. He wanted to know who was working where.

"I'm starting to understand how photographers and painters see," he said. Then his voice fell off some. "Wish I didn't feel so damn desperate." He sat up straight, cupped both hands around a match and lit a cigarette in one try in the windy cab.

"You okay for a quick stop in town, Butch?"

"Hell yes. You still living in your tent?" he chuckled.

"Where else."

"Could get crowded, Harp."

"Not for long. What I mean is ..."

Butch laughed. "Quit jumping through your ass. We'll both end up neurotic. We should make a few stops. Gotta hit the liquor store. How're you fixed for groceries?"

"Good on food. The liquor store's on the list."

"Got anything to read up there?"

"Oh, Playboys, Reader's Digests ..."

"Still reading magazines one-handed, huh?" he laughed, took a breath, then asked, "You find time to stir the pot with that tipi-maker these days?"

"I guess neither of us have been hungry enough to make the drive lately."

"Shit Harp, you wouldn't have to drive to Bend. Any of those long dress and hiking-booted gals in Corvallis would love to latch on to the notorious horse logger of Benton County."

"Yeah, nothing like the food stamp pioneers idealizing the mud ballet."

During the three years that Butch and I had worked together we'd talked a lot about the fascination some people had for the rain and mud and slippery side hills where we worked for our money. We might have cut as wide a swath through the ladies as we had in the woods, but the woods took a lot. Newspapers, a local television channel, and a national magazine had come to "cover" us at work. Butch had gotten a big kick out of it. "Profiling for the press," he called it. It was a life of the mind and of art we lived, it was a dance through slippery muck and knee-high brush, driving a team of fairly predictable horses, it was a slow sword fight with chainsaws, thinning out the lacy green canopy and letting daylight in the swamp. The media always depicted us as tough hippie loggers. We figured they were two-thirds correct.

We went into one of those two-acre stores that have everything and Butch bought a cot, a sleeping bag, a gas lantern, a red handled knife with about 40 tools in it, and a 120 dollar pair of binoculars. Then we stopped at the liquor store and he bought thirty-two bottles of Chivas Regal. It was all they had.

"Jesus, Butch."

"Well, what'm I gonna do — start a savings account?"

"Can I have the knife if anything happens to you?"

"You're adjusting nicely, Harp. Let's release these Chivas spirits into the clean air and begin the anesthesia. None of them hospital drugs can touch this stuff."

He had been one of those drinkers who stiffened and quickened his pace whenever he was drinking. He sounded game, but he was spent and sore. We had all we needed in town in two stops. His breathing was hard, loud, and painful by the time we got back on the road.

We hit my job site about an hour later, as the sunlight dimmed, the darkness congealed and the world went to black and white. Butch took in my headlight washed horse logging camp at a glance and nodded. Same old set up in a new place: Carbon and Buck were in a corral of rails spiked to trees in a rough rectangle. I'd nailed up some pole rafters and corrugated tin that kept their straw bedding dry. The crude roof drained into a bathtub. I fed them from a ton or so of three-wire grass hay bales I kept under clear plastic weighted down with some bald tires.

I pumped and lit a gas lantern on the picnic table and one in my tent. Butch graciously ignored me as I moved in his gear, the food, and the boxes of his favorite beverage. I cleared a space and set his cot up. He carried a lantern to the corral and Carbon and Buck snuffed and knickered at him, welcoming him back. Butch whispered back to them, making small, throaty sounds and breathing purposefully. When the tent was set up I went out and opened the hood on my pickup. I always kept cans of chili and soup on my exhaust manifold with hose clamps. I slammed the hood down and said "Supper." After a couple minutes Butch came in.

"Chili, huh?"

"I should poach a deer."

"How would ya cook him? On the motor?" he snorted, "Harp, sooner or later you gotta think of eating as more than something a body does to make a turd everyday."

I'd been eating engine-heated food for years. I enjoyed the homely feeling of standing outside the small grocery in Valsetz, up to my elbows in ticking V8 heat, fastening cans to my exhaust pipes with big hose clamps. "Warm's you up twice this way," I said.

Butch hunkered over his can of chili. His pearl snapped cowboy shirt that he'd filled only months ago was wrinkled and bunched over his shoulders.

"How's the job going? Looks like you got a winter's worth of saw logs decked up and waiting."

"Just drove by about forty loads and there's ten more or so decked on up the road. I've got maybe five or six on the ground to skid. Cherry pickin'. Easy money."

"Roadside contract?"

"Yeah. Too muddy to haul. That fat log-buyer of Yonko's eyeballs my decks from his windshield and pays me about half up front." I clapped the tent flaps together and our feet stilled under our respective cots.

"So yer flush?"

"Don't owe anybody either." I could dog it until the roads dried out and healed up some and I could get some self loading truckers to haul my logs. "The sun—remember that weird light in the sky?—it has to show up for a few days pretty soon." I said as we eased our wool-stock-inged feet out of our boots.

The hissing gaslight was too bright so I lit a few plumber's candles on a knee-high stool. We tin-cupped the Chivas, taking our time, and then forgot the cups. Outside, Carbon coughed and stomped. A light rain washed across the tent for a few minutes and quit. I squeezed shoe grease from a tube onto a pair of elk hide gloves and rubbed the stuff into Butch's boots, then did mine. When Butch passed the bottle I couldn't hold the tapered neck with the greasy gloves so he held it to my mouth. "One bubble, two bubbles," he said like a warning, and he lowered it.

"Harp, I'm lucky I'm here."

"Proud you knew where to come."

"Gonna be covering a lot of new ground," he said as he leaned back, fishing in his pants pocket. Butch opened his new pocketknife and tried the main blade on some wrist hairs. Then he held the blade a quarter-inch from the tip, lifted his beard, and pushed the point against his throat below his Adam's apple and nicked himself. "Think you could open up a choking guy's throat to save him? That's where you do it." He paused until I looked, "Thinnest place in the human skin ..."

"Jesus, Butch, go easy ..."

He furled his beard, hiding a scarlet rivulet that was headed down into his shirt. He stared at the candles. "It'll be weird at times. That's all."

I wrung the remaining grease into the gloves and threw them back under my cot.

"Pass the jug," I said. "And slow the shit show down."

He took a sloppy pull, wiped his dripping beard and said, "I want to die in the woods and let the coyotes and crows and bears and little bugs eat me. Little piles of ant shit."

He passed the Chivas and I wondered if I could somehow catch cancer from sharing the jug with him. He slowly opened and studied each blade of the new knife, fanning them at angles that left them all exposed. In the candlelight it looked like a lethal red and silver hand he'd been dealt. Then he collapsed them one by one.

"Harp, do you suppose if a goddamn coyote ate my lungs, he'd get cancer?"

"Jeez, you're reading my mind. But I don't know how to think about that," I answered, relieved at this turn of conversation.

"You know, you can skin a coyote and throw the carcass in a chicken coop and the chickens won't touch it. But they'll eat a skinned baboon. Remember old Wade?"

"You know, I never met Wade. How's the story go?" As if the stories about Butch and Wade weren't already local legend. I wanted to hear the one he had in mind, about Wade's last fight, and Butch knew it.

He cleared his throat, which took care and time. Memories of Wade preyed as hard on him as the crap he was hocking up. He spat a foamy pink loogie at the bottom edge of the door flap and settled into the story.

"Well, one of the sisters at the orphanage told me about a two-bit circus passing through Philomath that was missing a baboon. One drunk guy stayed on to look around for the baboon and the circus just split town. Sister Mary Algebra said he was a second-hand baboon and his 'provenance was uncertain,' but she figured he had to be real tame. This young nun knew I'd spent a lot of time walking logging roads and camping and acting like Boy Scouts with a couple other kids. I was sixteen and must've already spent three or four years in the Coast Range, roaming all summer. Anyway, I found the baboon. He was eating blackberries and kinda holed up in a thicket of them. I picked some mushrooms you can eat and he showed me some wild carrots that he even cleaned off. I showed him an old homestead with an orchard gone wild. We ended up staying in a banged up camp trailer some logger abandoned up on the Fathead pond campground. I worked here and there settin' chokers but mostly me and Wade roamed." He coughed humidly and launched another loogie at the flap.

"Spent a year together, more like fourteen or fifteen months. Ol' Wade ended up showing me every root, leaf, bug, and fungus you can eat in the Coast Range. Amazingly edible place around here. Came across Sasquatch families twice, but that's some other stories."

"Now how'd Wade end up skinned in Leo's chicken coop?"

Butch dumped a slash of Chivas down, tossed the lid at the tent flap, and said, "You know how old Deputy Leo limps. He was driving by our trailer and Wade was up on the roof tearing a worthless swamp cooler off. Leo stopped and banged on the door to tell me, as if I wouldn't know if I was home. Wade was just protecting his place. He jumped Leo and in the fight Leo's Achilles heel got bit off. Fight's a fight goddamnit, and Wade figured he'd won and he let Leo go. Leo crawled over to his County pickup and sat in it and started firing his Glock semi. He shot Wade about ten times. Goddamnit, I hate to think of poor Wade getting shot. He was real scared of guns. And that dip-shit Leo is a lousy shot. Skinned my little buddy and threw his carcass to the chickens. All those holes in the hide, but he had it tanned and hung it in his living room. Leo deserves to limp the rest of his miserable goddam life." Butch leaned over holding his head in his hands. "I miss Wade."

I'd never heard the story about Wade's demise with so few details. I blew out the candles.

It worries me when I should wake up feeling terrible, but don't. I'd just splashed horse water in my face and was reaching for my shirt and glasses when Butch emerged from the tent saying, "I had a dream that I was winning a foot race and when I broke the tape with my chest I knew in the dream I have lung cancer. What do you make of that?"

I've never thought once-off dreams are real important, but congratulated him on the race anyway. The scene in the tub distracted me. "Butch, look at this." I was squatting, with my glasses back on. He leaned over the tub holding his forehead with one hand.

A dead mouse floated in the whiskey-colored water. There were tiny scratches around and around the waterline scum in the tub.

Butch looked casually at the mouse, and then saw all the claw marks. He folded his arms over the lip of the tub and stared down at the drowned mouse.

A slice of dawn cut slowly, as it does in a rain forest under rolling clouds, right across Butch's back. He mused, "If you were a mouse and had the choice of falling in a tub and drowning or letting a cat play with you to death, what would you do?"

The rain that began pinging on our aluminum hardhats wasn't enough to keep us from starting, and we both wore waxed pants and slickers. I forked the horses a few flakes of hay, and we listened to the grinding resonance of their huge heads fill the shed. Butch rolled a cigarette with his elbows on the middle rail, his beard cushioning his chin on the top rail. His pallid hands looked uprooted. Watching Butch smoke made me want to smoke. It was ceremonial. He blew smoke rings out into the drizzle, unblinking as a burning tree.

Carbon hooked his tail like a quizzical eyebrow and some blind white worms writhed, suffocating in the steaming air around his turds. He was a good working horse. My failure to stop the worms in him was quenching his black coat. I'd had him wormed by the local vet monthly through the winter, with a long tube inserted up his nose. The worms seemed unfazed. His eyes and virility were still canny and he dominated the gelding, Buck, who outweighed him by six hundred pounds.

The rain gusted around us and I raised my voice.

"Let's sit in the pickup and have another cup."

"Why the hell not," he said, "I'll brew the mud while you warm her up."

We had the protocol down. As the engine got up to operating temperature, I gassed and oiled and filed my chainsaw on the tailgate. Butch walked up with a thermos and extra mug. When the tempo of a light rain dinging on an aluminum hardhat is suddenly multiplied by an area the size of a pickup roof, it sounds like it's raining about 50 times harder from inside the steamy, warm cab. We climbed in the idling truck. I ran the wipers to add to the atmosphere.

"Listen up, Harp It's picking up momentum."

"I could get some stuff down in between these lashings."

"You still gonna saw?" He asked. "Might get a little crazy. Wind's picking up. Isn't it?"

"Sure as hell," I agreed.

Butch leaned forward and wiped away some fog and looked up through the windshield at the tree tops for a bit and shook his head. "It's changing quarters, the tops are swirling."

"I oughta saw a few, see if they'll go where I want."

"They won't and you know it." he said. "Don't waste your time. How about shootin' pool?"

"Sounds safer. Where?" I was curious about where Butch would show himself.

"Tick's?"

"Yeah, nice tables there." It was a place loggers wouldn't usually go.

The coffee was about half Chivas. We drained the thermos on the drive down into town.

We drank a shot of top shelf whiskey at eight in the morning at Tick's and played a couple games of "bank-the-eight," but we got stalled. Scarred chair legs poked starkly at dim lights while the bartender mopped. The windowless, centrally heated ambiance of the place felt foreign. Both of us had spent most of our working lives outside, pretty much roofless all the time. We could drink in the morning to try to kill the pain but we couldn't do it indoors.

Back out in the parking lot we leaned over the back of my pickup, staring down at coldshuts, broken saw chains, feed buckets, and swollen spilled grain and Butch said, "Awkward, huh?" He reached in and grabbed the wraparound handlebar on my big McCulloch. He made a fist with his right hand and coughed and coughed into it while he held to the chainsaw. "Son of a bitch...son of a bitch" he said breathlessly as a prayer.

We drove aimlessly around Corvallis taking in how a rainy day could empty the sidewalks and parks. The whiskey glow dulled down and soured.

"Butch, you need to pick anything up?"

"I kinda do," he said. He shook as a spasm hit him. He composed himself and said evenly, "I should spend some time taking care of some stuff. You mind killing the afternoon?"

"Where can I drop you off?"

"Courthouse."

"They'll love to get their hands on you."

"You got any gum?" he said, and added, "Let's meet after quitting time at the Hoot Owl."

Under bowered maples, just starting to leaf out, he strode toward the courthouse in his logger's gait, a dying man with a baboon's bemusement. He was looking the trees over for possibilities. The sweatband in his hardhat had left a depression in his curly blond hair and he raked his fingers through it as though hoping to comply with some appearance code in government buildings.

I spent the afternoon under a bridge on the Mary's River. It was dry under there. A moldy trench coat and an empty Tokay bottle had been left next to a pillow of newspapers. The sibilant rush of the river would sound much louder and then it seemed to go nearly silent even though the flow looked unchanged. I thought I was losing touch with the reality of things right in front of me. I was projecting ahead, certain that the last of Butch was heading our way soon. He had misplaced his trust in my ability to help him take this step. I was going to let him down. I thought he must know that too. The tough and nonchalant routine wasn't going to last. My attitudes and my affectations were superficial. We'd both soon know how shallow and scared I was, and how worthless I'd be the worse things got. I turned away from the water and toward the newspaper pillow and the empty bottle. I wanted to follow the Tokay drinker, just hop a freight train and ride to somewhere sunny.

I squatted at the edge of the wash dangling my hands into the cold water wondering if a passive cleansing would occur, if without doing any wringing the grimy creases and calluses in my hands could come clean. Eventually, the thrumming of rush hour traffic overhead made me realize the time. I'd failed to figure out anything. An unspecific dread was the main emotion I carried out from under the Mary's River bridge. Butch was waiting under the sidewalk awning at the Hoot Owl.

Back in camp it was cloudy to the ground. The tent felt seedy and confining and we tacitly grabbed a jug and lantern and sat silently on hay bales under the shed roof.

Butch waved the Chivas towards my tent and said, "That's supposed to be a four man army tent?"

"Yeah," I said, reaching for the pitchfork.

"It could sure make four guys ready for a fight."

"Well it's a dry place to sleep and keep my stuff." I said, as I forked hay to the horses. Finished, I jammed the fork too hard into the end of the loose bale, it peeled a flake off and fell flat.

"Listen, Butch, I could tell you were serious about the coyotes and crows eating you, and it's high-minded of you – I mean, I admire the idea, but I've got to finish this job by June and I can't picture myself just ignoring the carrion, or whatever the hell is going to happen."

Butch stroked his beard upward and left his fingers in it. I could see the scab from his self-inflicted knife cut. He cleared his throat. "Two days, maybe three and there won't be anything casting shadows but my rib cage." He tried to laugh, coughed for quite awhile and said over the top of his bunched fist, "Harp, I know you thought I was serious. You sure look for heroes in weird places." He stood and stepped up to the corral rails. "Things clicked today: I've got some proper plans started with the county. Money don't talk, it lubricates."

Carbon snuffed at Butch's shirt pocket. He stood eye-to-eye with the black stud, scratching his roached mane while he pulled a plug of Day's Work out of his pocket. He bit off a chunk and gave it to the stud. Carbon raised his head and rolled his upper lip back exposing his pink and black mottled gums and long, yellowed teeth. Butch snorted and imitated Carbon but it looked to me like a grotesque parody. I went back to the tent. I'd finished greasing my boots when Butch came in with a couple cans of chili.

"Time to enjoy a meal," he said, as he cut the lid from a can with his new knife.

"You eat it. I'm cooking up a plan of my own. I'm taking off for Bend, to go see Caroline."

"Great idea. Key in the stock truck?"

"Yeah," I said. "Enough canned stuff on the exhaust to last a few days. Sorry."

"Kinda sudden ain't it," he said smiling down at a steaming spoon of chili. "What if I die while you're gone?"

"What if I get killed racing my hormones 120 miles over the Cascades?"

"See ya, bub. Take care of that gal." He reached over and grabbed my suspender and held it until our eyes met. "Harp, you're better at all this than you know. Give Caroline a squeeze and a half for me."

The lights were still on in Caroline's workshop at nine o'clock. Her dusty El Camino was parked next to the only tree around, a shaggy-barked juniper; its lower reaches decorated with empty birdcages. In the long tin shed she had built 50 foot tables where she rolled around 45-pound bolts of canvas. She could cut seven layers at a time. She had pulled miles of canvas through her big sewing machines and made hundreds of tipis in her tin shed on the Tumalo Flats. She shipped out enough tipis to buy time to spend with her saddle horses.

Butch and I had met her at a horse show. We'd been walking sort of walleyed down the middle of some rows of horse trailers, many with horses tied to them eating hay off the tailgates. When you're amongst horses' asses you notice everything, and we both noticed Caroline and this wound-up chestnut mare struggling. Caroline was easy to look at, cowgirl-firm with a plait of bleach-streaked and ginger hair thick as her wrist that dangled to her waist. She was trying everything that patience and good horsemanship would suggest, and then some, but that mare wouldn't walk up the ramp into the trailer. Butch walked over and offered to help. Caroline said something like she'd "sell the goddamn mare for five bucks," or worse. She backed off and Butch hooked a finger in the mare's halter. Butch stood facing the way the mare looked, not making eye contact, and Caroline and I could see his lips moving but heard nothing. Caroline stood by silently, her hands grabbing her ass from inside her back pockets. Then Butch and the mare walked into the trailer. After a couple of minutes he walked back down the tailgate, looked over his shoulder and said, "There's too many good horses in the world to put up with that. She's stupid mean. I'd take cannery price if she was mine."

Caroline was set back by this whole scene and pronouncement, but she was cool enough to have a beer with us. With Caroline between us we lounged on Butch's hood against his windshield watching a smoky Oregon sunset diffuse like bruises drifting to sea. We talked about some of the idiocy of horse shows. Caroline connected horses to Saturn, but didn't sound too dogmatic about it. Butch talked up his plan about heading back to Alaska.

Before she left, the hairs on our arms brushed a few times and we both made promises we'd damn sure keep.

This was the fourth time in seven months that I'd made the trip over the Cascades to see her.

She set down her scissors and gave me one of those limp new presses that are supposed to pass for hugs.

"Harp, I am absolutely swamped. I'm so far behind ... You should have phoned."

"Caroline. Slow down."

"That's easy for you to say. You've got Carbon and that ugly gelding to help you." She sniffed and looked at me sideways, "Sorry," she shrugged. "Truth. What all brings you to the desert?"

"Butch is back, he needs a tipi."

"I'm backed up about six weeks."

She clenched her jaw unconsciously, her slightly overshot upper lip pouted. She had turned halfway around back towards her work when I said, "He has cancer in both lungs. It'd be a place for him to live until he dies."

Her tanned hands splayed against the white canvas, her shoulders squeezed together. She spoke down at the workbench, "How old ... how long ..?"

"Thirty-one, goddamnit, thirty-one, and he's dying and it isn't going to stop, or even take very long now." I found myself crying and speaking at once, making sounds I'd never in my life heard coming from my throat.

She turned and whispered against my chest, "What a strange, abrupt cycle," and held me for a good while.

We both eventually drew in a few breaths and she said, "He needs an amulet and a tipi. You stay here tonight."

Her tiny pine house was lofty and tidy. Two walls were given to shelves of books and photographs. In one photograph she was hellbent on a quality bay polo-pony, her mouth and eyes set in lines straight and purposeful as the mallet she swung alongside her head. Bird wings and prisms hung from threads in the south window. Fabrics, clothing and blankets were folded into patterns of color and texture up at the end of the sleeping loft.

She lit some candles, seated us on tan corduroy pillows, and closed her eyes. After a couple of minutes she got a cigar box off the shelf behind her and took an eagle skull out and plucked tiny feathers from between its eyes. She laid them on a wisp of mountain goat fur and then took out some clay from a famous arch in Greece. She spit on these things and worked the clay with the feathers and fur in it into a ball, then into a snake shape. From the cigar box she took a pink sliver of wood, it was the heartwood from a Ponderosa pine that had been struck by lightning and scarred to the ground, but lived on. She wound the clay-and-fur-and-feathered snake around the sliver, in a tapered ascending spiral, and then stuck it into an odd shaped piece of black leather with fine, sparse hair on it. It was a piece of brain-tanned Percheron scrotum from a stud I had gelded. She was the only woman I'd ever met who I knew would appreciate such a gift. Before she sewed it shut, she handed it to me and said, "Think something uplifting about Butch, then spit your snoose in there." She sewed it shut and said, "That's the kind of sewing I should be doing."

"Yeah, well, its all women's work," I replied, hoping the playfulness in my voice would redeem me.

"Up yours, tree killer," she said and rose from her pillow graceful as campfire smoke.

She made a minty-smelling herb tea and we settled into the candlelight.

We eased into the idea of Butch dying. I'm edgy about new age pretensions but, in truth, she was studious about death. She pulled out books by names like Ouspensky, Gurdjieff, and Blavatsky, in which she'd underlined lots of passages. She read from a thick white book with a blue target and the word Urantia on the cover. We talked through the night, or she taught and I listened. For hours we strolled the desert, avoiding bitter brush and creeping juniper by the light of the stars. She wound the Milky Way, seashells, pine cones and all the natural spirals of the universe into DNA, which she said was naturally of the same geometry. The intensity and sureness of her beliefs got through as much as what she was giving me to understand. What turned me around during that night was her truehearted serenity about death as a moving point on the unending spirals. During that long night I learned to trust cycles and knew that what had just transpired would stick and that Butch's life would resonate infinitely. I believe her still.

At sunup Caroline put the candle stubs back into the box with the eagle skull. We cooked eggs. We carried buckets to Tumalo Creek and back the 200 paces to her garden and then corralled her quarter horse and prancy Morgan mare and she kicked fine-stemmed first cut flakes from alfalfa bales under the low rails. She plucked off their braided halters and we watched her mares get down to business.

I wandered away and squatted awkwardly at her pit privy nursing a New-Age mind hangover into gratitude. Instead of being under the bridge, confused, counting losses, awash in uncertainty, I felt like I was on the bridge. Images of me doing good by Butch, and him knowing that, were somehow of a piece.

Back at her shop she helped me load up a brand new 18 foot diameter tipi, liner, and rain fly; a gift for Butch. We made promises as dear as those first ones from the fairgrounds parking lot.

Hugs can be long bear hugs that leave you with some certainty. We hugged.

Caroline said in the wake of a sigh. "Harp, be good to yourself. Be strong."

"I'll be back soon, real soon, to spend some time."

"You pay close attention." Her eyes searched back and forth from one of mine to the other.

"Well, when this thing's done I'll bring some dynamite over and make you a ten foot deep outhouse hole. Hey, we could call it the *Butch Memorial Powder Room*."

"I'll feed you. Give Butch my love."

"He'll know all about it. You are one good woman Caroline."

"Sweet-talking tree killer. Go setup that tipi."

When I got back to camp, the stock-truck tailgate was still down. Buck was fed. Carbon and Butch were gone. I cut and skinned fifteen tipi poles from some three-inch fir saplings, dog hair trees with little taper in the first twenty feet. The sun on my arms made them look akin to the trees I was working with. Peeling poles that smooth is sculpture.

I had erected tipis a few times using a book that had photographs of a 1950 Studebaker sedan, with tipi-poles lashed to it. The book gave a simple and exact description of a process that would have tempted many a writer to more flowery stuff. Just the step-by-step and bits of anecdotal folklore.

I threw a proper clove hitch around the three main poles in the first try. The lift pole with the tipi cover attached featured a horsetail pennant that Buck wouldn't miss until fly-time.

Big taut pure white cone in the woods.

I'd just gotten a fire going in there and was settling down on the canvas ground cloth when I heard Butch letting Carbon back into the corral. He hunched over and stepped through the oval door of the tipi and slowly straightened up. He took it in, looked up, down, and around with the fire building and pulsing light on him.

"Man alive. One of Caroline's?"

"Yeah... gift. She sends her love and this amulet."

"A tent with a fire inside," he said, "Them Indians were on their way." It was bright and getting warm in there, and Butch peeled off a couple of sweatshirts. He studied the hairy black amulet with his head cocked to let the cigarette smoke past his eyes and he hung it around his neck without knocking the ash off his smoke. The fire burned surely. Aromatic cedar and cigarette smoke convected swiftly up and out the center hole to the unseen sky.

"Caroline, oh Caroline," Butch effused.

"How'd you and Carbon do?" I'd never known anyone who went on unfettered walks with a horse. The day was mostly up to the horse.

Butch would just hang around with him all day. Sometimes sitting on him, unbridled, or standing listening, or foraging alongside him for the stuff that Wade had taught him to eat.

"Harp, old Carbon has about as much time left as I do."

"I don't think he's that bad," I said, knowing he was right.

"Every good horse is a broken heart."

We spent most of the next several weeks sipping Chivas Regal. I worked a day here and there when Butch went to town. The tipi was the ascending vortex of our meals and drinking and talking inside that cone of light. Butch pulled the amulet from under his shirt sometimes and held it like a small bird, then let it drop back against his chest. We spent some days walking and resting on the stumps of jobs we'd done over the years. New growth was twice as tall as we were in the old cuts. Butch showed me things Wade had taught him. It got harder for him to get around, and he used the binoculars more. I kept the windows on the pickup clean. Then it got to the point where I'd make him a sort of sleeping bag nest and then had to help him out of the pickup to piss.

It was cold and calm the morning after we finished that last jug of Chivas. I poked my head in Butch's tipi. He looked puny – the standup force of his life in the woods had been reduced to the small struggle of rolling a cigarette with his stringy arms sticking out of his sleeping bag. While he smoked, I built a fire and split up more kindling.

"Krusteaz and cackle berries?"

"Suit yourself." He dressed and went outside awkwardly. When I finished eating, the sun was up, but not warming up yet. He was at the corral staring down into the water tub, and then he began whispering to Carbon.

"Good luck, old man," I heard him say as I walked over.

I'd never heard him speak to Carbon in English before.

"Goodbye, Harp." He stood there with his fists in his pockets, hunched over. "There's an envelope in there under my pillow. Two, in fact."

"You're not done yet ... I didn't think it was that bad."

"It's that bad."

I reached for him with both arms.

"No hug Harp. I'd break," and he offered some eye contact that he held straight faced. "I'll be leaving the stock truck at Stan's saw shop in Newport."

We went quiet while he leaned over catching his breath. He looked up and said, "Pretty decent time in my life," and some bloody slobber escaped his mouth and dripped straight down. He kind of choked and added, "Thanks for the memories." And he smiled sideways like he'd told a one-liner.

He threw my hip-waders in the stock truck cab and drove away without adjusting the mirror.

The red-handled knife, binoculars, and envelopes were under his pillow. A piece of paper folded in half that said "Harp" on it said to go to Baboon Ridge and dig a grave next to where Wade's bones were buried. It said it would be marked with surveyor's stakes with blue ribbons. I was then to "proceed," he wrote, to the Yaquina Bay Coast Guard station with the tipi cover.

The gravesite, as well as about a sixty foot circle around it, was clearly staked and flagged. The ground turned rocky about three feet down. Stupidly, I piled the rocks on top of the soft soil from the top of the hole. At about five feet, after four mindless hours, I squared the edges, leveled the bottom and climbed out. I went back to camp, changed into a clean shirt and stripped the smoke darkened tipi cover off of the poles, and headed for Newport.

Butch had flicked himself off the Yaquina Bay bridge.

When I got to the Coast Guard they directed me to the county coroner's. I introduced myself to him and gave him the envelope. It had three different letters in it. Butch had been busy on those trips to town. The coroner shook his head slowly. He looked up, experimenting with lamentable facial expressions.

"According to these papers, copies of which I received just yesterday, you are here to claim the body of one Edwin P. Brim. I am familiar with the law here, but I called the County Attorney and he was actually anticipating my call. This is extraordinary."

He handed me a piece of paper to sign. Butch's middle name was Percival, a name that struck me as heroic, and I figured that the orphanage nuns must have named him.

"If I can have him, would you help me with something?" We spread out Caroline's tipi cover, which infused the pale green tiled hallway with its campfire smell. We lowered Butch off a gurney, and rolled him up in it while I tried not to see his face. I carried him out to my pickup and sat him in the cab like I'd done for the last couple weeks. The coroner brought out a sodden box full of Butch's wet clothes and my waders. I climbed in the cab and reached over and rested him against my shoulder.

Back at Baboon Ridge I laid Butch next to the hole and rigged a rope around him and lowered him. I dropped the rope in the hole and sorted out the rocky backfill so all I scooped were handfuls of soft dirt on his shroud. When I couldn't see the canvas anymore I cleaned my glasses and started backfilling with the shovel. Then I walked over to the edge of a patch of spruce and dug up a bunch of saplings. I planted thirteen of them in a spiral from the edge of the blue-flagged circle in to the grave. As the sun set, I planted one right on top of Butch.

Old Carbon died a couple weeks later.

I went back up to Baboon Ridge last summer. The tree on Butch's grave was six feet taller than the others. I picked a cone off it. Feeling its corkscrewed scales my thoughts spun back to other vortices; seashells, the Milky Way, DNA, spirals of tipi fabric, and the rolling of cigarettes.

A Matter of Degrees

(published in several big city newspaper Sunday editions.)

Author note: In 1989 I arranged to get a ride up the Alyeska pipeline haul road from Fairbanks to Prudhoe Bay, in the dead of winter and I ran head first into this jackpot.

In Fairbanks, Alaska, on January 30, 1989, the air temperature never got above 56 below zero. The night before, a Canadian military C-130 had crashed while trying to land at Wainwright Army Base, killing the crew of eight. The tragedy was blamed on the effects of the record-breaking cold on the Hercules aircraft engines. Word at the airport was that the fuel had gelled and the turbines died on final approach. My 737 ride into Fairbanks was the last flight to get in for the next 8 days.

Ice fog so thickly shrouded the town along the Chena river, a major tributary of the Yukon, that I couldn't tell when walking across an intersection if there were vehicles coming or not. Multiple car pile-ups were common, vehicles were abandoned where they'd broken down and the Fairbanks hospital and clinics were treating dozens of ill-clad motorists for frostbitten extremities after they had tried to walk for help. Fan belts shattered by the cold kept appearing at my feet. The sunbleached sign for the Cheechako Inn bragged "Electric Heat," which was an attribute I'd appreciated as I walked the mile across town the motel owner had warned me to not try. Two layers of fleece long-johns, 40 below boots, boiled wool pants, a huge green down "Michelin man" coat and a beaver skin hat were adequate for strolling atop the crunchy snowpack.

Earlier that day the Alaska State Department of Transportation had officially closed the 516 mile all-weather road from Fairbanks to the Prudhoe Bay oilfields. For the first time in its ten year history, the remote road through the Alaska interior was deemed unsafe due to extreme cold. I'd come to Fairbanks to take a ride north on the Pipeline Haul Road and was at best ambivalent about heading even farther into the Arctic and colder temperatures. I reached the trailer house office of the Sourdough Express to meet Whitey Gregory the garrulous driver/owner figuring he'd be telling me my ride up north would be postponed.

The vast, fenced, Sourdough Express truckyard was notable for its dozens of street lights, their pink sodium-vapor glow barely prevailed over the ice fog. The yard was replete with a couple dozen quiet semi tractors that were clean of snow and an array of variously configured trailers, most being tankers. I walked into the cavernous shop with Whitey who told me that if he was to open one of the 14 foot high doors enough, heat would escape and fluids in the shop would freeze before the furnace could raise the temperatures back up to normal. "Normally," Whitey, verbose and warm hearted, declared "it's too cold to snow." He cut a chuckle short and added, "Get it?"

About then, an average-sized man lumped up in arctic coveralls stomped in from the yard while flapping his arms against each other. He pulled off his electric blue stocking cap. With an economic but histrionic ascending twirl he unwound a hunter's orange scarf as ice crystals fell and settled on the concrete floor. His face looked sculpted by high winds; long brown hair combed straight back over the top of his head, a salty auburn beard parted at the chin and swept earward, and a raptor's squint. "My eyebrows froze out there in two minutes," he said. "This weather is appalling."

I was introduced to Clay Gustaves, a 41 year old freelance trucker who was picking up one of Whitey's tank trailers to make an emergency run to the Kuparuk oilfield, west of Prudhoe Bay, with a load of de-icing methanol. He went back out into the 3:00 P.M. darkness rasping, "Tires." in his Camel-smoker voice.

Whitey Gregory explained that the state D.O.T. agreed to let this one trucker try to haul the 8,000 gallons of methanol to the North Slope because the need for it as a de-icer for the oil rigs constituted an emergency. None of the salaried Sourdough Express drivers would pull the inflammable load in the prevailing weather conditions, so Gustaves had been contracted to haul it with his independently owned Freightliner. Whitey told me that this driver has never had an accident in more than 900 trips during his nine years plying the Haul Road. Clay Gustaves' unblemished driving record spanned the ten year history of the haul road and was already legendary. His 1983 Freightliner had 660,000 miles on it, all of them earned on the 1,000+ mile round-trip on the unpaved road from Fairbanks to the oilfields. In this, his last week before he was to take a year off, he wanted all the trips he could get. Whitey glanced at me sideways and said he didn't like the idea of a truck out there alone in this, but figured if anyone could make it, Clay would. "By whatever means, they just plain got to have their methanol to keep the rigs running up there." Whitey cleared his throat as he studied the floor. Then his florid face brightened a bit and he suggested that if I were willing to risk it, I could ride with Clay. He said if the D.O.T. objected to a passenger having gone on the trip, he'd smooth things out later. "I'm not trying to talk you into anything, but the road's never been closed before," Whitey enthused. He sounded borderline envious. "You'll be the only truck on it. This is a chance to see something real unusual."

Gustaves stomped back in, said the trailer was secured to his tractor, and regarded Whitey as though he was waiting for something. Whitey warned me that during the 500 mile trip north it would only get colder, and that a breakdown could be deadly since there would be no other truckers around to help. If the truck got stuck, but the engine could still run, the heaters in the cab would keep us alive. However, if the extreme cold caused the diesel fuel to gel, or if we hit a moose or anything else and damaged the radiator, the diesel engine would die and we'd be stranded without heat. A propane-fueled heater would be useless because at about 42 below zero, liquid propane freezes, it gets too thick to flow like a gas. I suggested that if we did have to spend time without the truck's heat, we could just dig a snow cave and wait it out. But Clay told me that much of the land north of the Arctic Circle is arctic desert. Even though it is all white up there, "Dry snow does not readily lend itself to making an igloo," Clay explained. "The same snow just blows hither and yon all winter, it gets beat up and it has the structural integrity of sugar, my friend."

Whitey added another caveat: since aircraft altimeters are calibrated to barometers, and since the record-breaking cold was accompanied by barometric pressure readings that were higher than barometers are commonly built to record, there was no way to calibrate the altimeters, all aircraft in Alaska were grounded indefinitely. "Nobody's flying until it warms up to thirty below," Whitey declared. There would be no possibility of any rescue-by-aircraft should we not arrive in Prudhoe Bay when expected. "You will truly be on your own up there," he said.

A vague notion that there must be some way to stay warm when hauling 8,000 gallons of inflammable fluids flickered through my head. I was dimly intuiting some kind of inchoate story about Arctic survival.

Gustaves shifted his weight under all his layers of clothing. He was pacing around the office, anxious to get on the road. He said he'd always wanted to drive the only truck in the Arctic. "Make it or not, my friend, this is the real deal. We'll be riding point and cleanup on the northernmost escape from inertia in the world." He slowed down, "It is unimaginably gorgeous up there. All the way." The clarity and promise of that short speech seduced me as if spoken by a wily fugitive from a world that strives to eliminate chance. He looked me over and added, "Your costume suggests that you are prepared to proceed." I agreed.

Despite the urgency about delivering the methanol, we sat five-miles north of Fairbanks at the Hilltop truck stop for more than an hour while Rosy, the owner, made sacks full of sandwiches and poured coffee for bundled figures hunched over the dun counter. She told us about a film crew from L.A. that had been stranded up near Coldfoot for a few hours the day before. The tame wolves they brought for the film resisted leaving the vans to go out in the cold. When they did set foot out of their cages, they tried to stand on one foot at a time. Finally, the story went, the film crew agreed with the wolves' survival instincts, but by then none of their vans would start and they were stranded. A trucker found them several hours later and packed the whole crew into his cab and sleeper and took them to Fairbanks. They had all been flown to Providence Hospital in Anchorage where they were losing toes to frostbite. A few of the guys had heard this story. No one asked what became of the wolves.

Rosy fretted at Clay while packing our lunches, saying she couldn't believe we were trying this. She gave us extra cookies and fruit and said the oilfields shouldn't need the de-icing fluid anyway. The pipeline flow was slowed down because three-feet of snow and 80 mile per hour winds at the terminal down at Valdez were preventing oil tankers from sailing. Clay chided Rosy, saying she knew more about the pipeline flow than her own blood pressure. She waved a dishrag in front of her face at nothing, reminded him to buy his three packs of Camels for the trip, and we left.

By 3:00 P.M. the sun had set, the temperature at the Fairbanks North weigh station was 67 below zero as we rolled onto the scales and weighed in right at 99,000 pounds. Clay did a walk around, thumping all 26 tires with a billyclub while listening for any variations in the dull thuds. He clanged the club against the 8,000 gallon tank once and said he likes hauling fluids. The tank trailers have internal baffles, but "The surging and splashing back there still goes on and adds another dimension to the job." "A 'wet' load," Clay winked, "becomes a live influence on a trip up that snaky old Haul Road."

The road heading north from Fairbanks to Livengood is officially called the Elliot Highway. Haul road truckers call the first 40 miles "Moose Alley." Moose tracks pock the angel food surface. Moose prefer walking the smooth road to weaving through the dense, scrubby white spruce and alder woods that crowd the roads. Snow removal crews blade down the berm of plowed snow at the road's edge so the moose can get off the road when trucks are using it. We saw several. They strolled the road's center, magnificently possessing their territory while ignoring us.

There isn't a straight, level mile on the 70 mile road to Livengood. Clay constantly changed gears as we drove down into and back out of dozens of drainages and tributaries with names that chronicle various cultural incursions into the Alaska interior: Chatanika, Tatalina, Tolovana, Amy, Fossil, and Heine, to name a few. A red digital readout on the dashboard flashed outside temperatures. In the low places, where the cold settles, 74 below zero was the rule. The hilltops and high plateaus warmed up to 65 below.

At mile 62, still south of Livengood, the rubber seal on my door had shrunk from the cold enough to allow the door to pop open. We stopped, and Clay used some, "100 mile per hour tape," (duct tape) to connect a piece of heater-hose to the defroster. After blowing warm air on the seal for half an hour, the door would stay shut. "Victory is mine, sayeth Clayborn," he announced. "Any trip on the Haul Road is more of a project than a drive." Then he added, "Please don't use your door unless you have to jump."

In a few miles, we came to the first 16 percent grade, (passenger-car roads rarely exceed 6 percent). Clay told me to grab my coat and be ready to jump. If the wheels start to slip on a steep grade, the truck can "spin out," lose momentum, and stop. The warm tires immediately turn the snowpacked surface to ice, and the truck will slide backward uncontrollably. If that happened, we would both have to jump and hope the truck wasn't wrecked. "The trick to jumping properly," Clay coached me, "is to jump pretty far out there so you don't slide back under the truck. Make it a good jump."

After several more hills like that, hills on which I kept my coat on my lap and a grip on my door handle, Clay stopped at the top of Hess hill to relax. "Take charge a little," he called it. Walking around the truck, we found the first shattered tire. Jagged edges showed where shards of tread and sidewall rubber, bigger than a handprint, had cracked off. Clay said he'd never seen a tire shatter like that. It was 50 miles to the Yukon Bridge truck stop where we could replace it.

We climbed back in the cab, and he shifted back up through the gears again. The nine-speed and four-speed transmissions were a mystery to me in the dim green glow of the dashboard lights. I couldn't discern the patterns and combinations of his shifts through the two transmissions. But in the constantly varying terrain we traversed, his gear shifting comprised a strategy that anticipated every hill, curve, and approaching straightaway before they appeared in the headlights. There was nothing incomplete about Clay's knowledge of what was coming and his preparation for it. There was never a lapse in his anticipation. He drove in possession of a 516 mile long memory of every feature and nuance of the Haul Road. After failing to plumb the mysteries of the transmissions, I did try to keep track of how many times he changed gears. I estimated that that he was shifting gears about 6 times every mile.

By 11:30 P.M. we'd made the first 150 miles and reached the Yukon river bridge, a 2,900 foot long concrete-railed ramp descending from south to north. We drove down into an ice fog so well defined it looked like we'd feel the truck enter it. High-intensity sodium-vapor lights are spaced every 100 feet along the length of the bridge. We could only see two sets of lights ahead of us.

Toby Williams, 65, the manager of Yukon Bridge Ventures was in his shop, but surprised there was a truck on the Haul Road this night. Toby has a bad back and he had no hired help on hand. We now had three shattered tires to replace, and Clay also discovered that the main U-joint to the drive axles was loose. There were no replacement U-joints big enough to fit the Freightliner at Yukon Bridge, but Clay decided we could make it to Coldfoot and see if they had one. We changed the shattered tires out next to the building in a series of ten-minute efforts that weren't physically exhausting, but left us breathless from trying to get the job done without sucking in much of the arctic air. Thankfully, there wasn't a puff of wind. The twin chrome exhaust-stacks pushed diesel plumes hard at the crystallized air. The interface, where fumes met ice fog, looked as plainly drawn as two hot-air balloons inflating.

While the truck idled at Yukon Bridge the gear-lube in the transmissions and differential nearly solidified. When we got the load moving again, the U-joint withstood the engine's tremendous torque and the resistance of the frozen lubricants clotting the drive train. As we drove back onto the road again, the gearshifts were nearly impossible for Clay to manipulate. He drove for six or seven miles at a crawl to allow the lubricants to loosen up.

Then, during our deliberate ascent up the three-mile hill called the Beaverslide, he put his hand to his left ear as though listening to something gone wrong and said, "Oh no. Why didn't I check it back at Yukon Bridge? There's no turning back now." I involuntarily grabbed my coat and the door handle as I tried to hear the problem. But his concern was for the clasp for his diamond earring that had fallen off while changing tires. "Personal rigging losses on the tough old Haul Road." he laughed.

In the relative quiet of the slow going up Beaverslide, he told me that some truckers won't stop at Yukon Bridge because the word is out that a religious cult bought the place. But he thinks that living at that outpost will keep them humble. He talked about his father teaching him to drive big rigs in a log truck in Idaho 25 years ago—the same truck that killed his dad. Now he believes his father watches over him, keeping him safe. We both spoke of fathers prematurely dead, and our ongoing faith in their protective powers that has let us both be strangely tempted by abnormal doings.

At 1:30 A.M. we reached the top of Baker's Knob on the backbone of the Ray Mountains. Clay needed sleep, but insisted I use the sleeper behind the cab. He set an alarm for 5:30 A.M. and fell asleep hunched over the steering wheel. Every screw visible in the sleeper was thickly coated with frost wicked through layers of sheet metal, insulation, and the padded leather walls.

When the alarm went off, Clay was leaning against the window. His hair was frozen to it. He pulled himself away from the ice-encrusted glass, and we got out to stretch and walk around the truck. The idling motor had nothing more to do while we slept than keep the cab heaters blasting. It was 155 degrees colder outside the truck. We found two more shattered tires. The Coldfoot Camp truck stop was another 100 miles north.

Again we crawled down the road, letting the running gear loosen up. At about 6:00 A.M. a Fairbanks radio station announced it was 74 below zero there. The state of emergency declared by the Governor was still in effect. All records for low temperatures in Alaska had been broken. The announcer asked that all non-essential workers stay home. "How would you like to decide for yourself that you're non-essential?" Clay wondered out loud, as the 50-ton load he was causing to move through the arctic began to limber-up and live again.

By the time we climbed and descended another half-dozen valleys, the side windows were opaque with frost and less than half the area of the windshield was clear. In our headlights, the thousands of spruce trees we passed were totally coated with ice, not a limb or suggestion of bark visible. Alders were bent under their wind-driven loads of ice like Bigfoot snares. Forsaken and wild as the place appeared, Clay said he wanted to ride his Harley Davidson to that eerie, hostile ridge called Gobbler's Knob and park it and watch the sun set behind it with the toothy spikes of black spruce profiled behind.

Farther down the road, after driving along the narrow spine of the Kanuti Mountains for 35 miles, we crossed the Arctic Circle. At that moment we were laughing over a tape of Robin Williams explaining how God designed the platypus.

Between the Arctic Circle and Stormy Hill, the Northern Lights began to wash greens and golds across the entire sky. The frost-occluded side-windows and windshield edges pulsed dully with the light, but where the defroster kept the glass clear it was a sight to widen the eyes of the weariest traveler. Under the ethereal glow we drove by a trailer loaded with structural steel, abandoned on the side of the road. It was the first of several forsaken loads we would pass on the way to the North Slope. Clay said the poor soul hauling that load just unhooked it a few days ago, drove back to Fairbanks bobtail, and quit. He talked about drivers killed or just psychologically wrecked by the Haul Road as we drove alongside Bonanza Creek over hundreds of fresh moose tracks. He said that for the last 50 miles we had been driving on top of four or five feet of accumulated ice and snow. "This road works on extremes," he said. "It builds up and you think the jackpot is getting bigger. Then these drivers decide for themselves that the loads are all millstones, and it's all tragedy instead." He held me with a look that kept his eyes off the road for a couple of seconds.

The next wide spot in the road Clay called, "Happy Man." It is named after a fellow who lived there alone in a camp trailer for a few years. He had a portable air compressor and the rudiments of the tire repair business and he fixed flats for 80 dollars apiece. With normal traffic running to over 100 trucks per day, he did a terrific cash business and always seemed to smile.

As we drove along, most of our conversations were short and yelled. Talk happened as an adjunct to Clay's occupation. He never allowed himself more than a quick glance away from the road, and he was never idle. The steering wheel is as big as the top of a cocktail-lounge table, and about as horizontal. He constantly corrected our course, riding with most of his torso bent over the big wheel. Clay wasn't just driving; he was using all his limbs, his extremities, like a veteran athlete competing in a game in which the rules can change instantly. At its roomiest, the road gives drivers 32 feet of width to work with. We had already seen dozens of places in the roadside ice berms where a driver had deviated a few feet and got sucked down into the ditch.

As we neared Aleyska Pipeline Company Pump Station Five, in the Prospect Creek drainage, we came across another truck. The red Kenworth, with a tank trailer attached, was idling in a turnout. Clay explained it was a company truck that ferried fuel to three pump stations along a 200 mile length of the pipeline. He stopped to make a "courtesy call." Clay knocked on the locked door, but no one answered. He showed me wolf tracks laid over that truck's tire imprints in the snow. It was 8:30 A.M. and the sodium-vapor glow from the big array of pump station lights half a mile away cast a roseate blush on the white hills and trees around the trucks in the uncut Arctic darkness.

Clay turned his C.B. radio on and called the Pump Station Five security as we pulled back onto the spruce-lined road. A woman's voice responded immediately. He asked her the temperature. "Negative Seventy-Eight." came the terse reply. Clay quipped, "Think about summer, darlin'." Between shifts he tugged the cellophane wrapper on the hula-dancer air freshener hanging from a dashboard knob. Cloying coconut scent insinuated itself on the cab like some redolent Malaysian fantasia.

Near Gold Bench, as the Freightliner growled up out of the south fork of the Koyukuk River, Clay pointed ahead at a saddle-shaped mountain in the moonless night. A barely visible white slash cut over the swell above the seat. The faint slash was the longest, steepest, most intimidating grade yet. "If we make this hill, it's overdrive to Coldfoot and coffee," Clay sang. Midway up the long climb, the hill gets steeper. Where the road might have turned and cut across the seat of the saddle-mountain, instead, it heads straight up over the swell of the saddle.

The all-weather road, from the Yukon River to Prudhoe Bay, was built in one year. It demands the upper limits of diesel-tractor capabilities as well as mighty levels of human skill. Theoretically, it is always possible to pull a load on it without using tire chains, the colder snow gets, the harder its crystalline structure, until it's like driving on packed sugar. But the contingencies crop up, and are mortally threatening. The road, where it steepened, was rutted, gouged, and icy from many recent spinouts. Clay dropped down a gear, and steered the truck right out to the edge of the ruts and icy tracks and then a bit farther, where the snow was virgin and traction might be better. "If this doesn't work, I'll be wanting to jump out your side," he barked. Just out his door was a drop into abysmal darkness. The eight drive-tires caught and Clay pulled fifty tons to the top without needing to downshift. At the summit, he stopped and we got out. He didn't bother with his coat, but stomped around silently on the verge of the road, cigarette sticking from the dead center of his parted beard. He blew gouts of smoke as he looked down at the narrow edge he'd just used to make it up the hill. Then he declared he loves, just loves, this job. He can't believe they pay him to live such a life.

We found two more shattered tires on the trailer up there. When we got back in the cab, I asked what were the chances we'd break a front tire. "Chances are," he said. "Then what?" I asked. Clay said he'd probably be trying to steer right up to the point we wrecked. There are 24 wheels on the truck that can only go straight. If you lose one of the two that steer, you can't control anything with 99,000 pounds pushing you where it will. He said he hoped I wasn't stressed out.

I thought back to ten years of timber falling and using explosives during my logging career in the Pacific Northwest, and about how seldom fear had ever helped. I had decided that trust in yourself, the people you work with and in good equipment was the key to a life that constantly holds your interest. "I wish I'd have tried that," is an awfully tragic admission once it's too late.

We reached Coldfoot by 9:00 A.M. and were met by Dick Mackey, who won the 1,049 mile long Iditarod sled dog race in 1978. He and his wife, Cathy, put the winnings down to start the "Northernmost Truckstop in the World," as his hat says. A school bus with a plywood shed attached served as the first cafe. Ten years later they have an airstrip, a truck-repair shop, a 100-seat cafe, a real home, and 160 beds in refurbished pipeline buildings that they bought cheap and hauled to Coldfoot. The energy bill for their businesses now runs about $125,000 per year. The entire operation at Coldfoot is a fossil fuel-based microcosm. It's the midway-point between Fairbanks and Prudhoe Bay, the last place on the road to buy necessities. They don't sell gasoline. There has never been a call for car fuel that far north.

The day before, Dick Mackey had been interviewed over telephone a number of times by media from around the world. His thermometer had become famous. It is calibrated down to 80 below zero, but yesterday the mercury fell past the last mark and settled in the bulb at the bottom. Dick said his measurements were unofficial, but he was calling it 81 below. He then took me and my steaming cup of coffee out in the parking lot for my "Cheechako Initiation." He told me to throw the coffee up in the air. I did, and heard soft popping and cracking sounds, like a whole bowl of Rice Krispies going off at once. A tan cloud of flash-frozen coffee crystals drifted away. Not a drop made it to the ground. The thermometer on the outside of the cafe had crept up to an honest 79 below zero.

Dick Mackey still raises and races sled dogs, as does his son, Rick, who won the Iditarod in 1983. A dog sled hangs from the vaulted ceiling of the Coldfoot cafe. Dick reckons he has put over 20,000 miles on that sled, mushing the Alaska interior with a fervor for wilderness and his half-wild dogs that possibly derives from the heroic landscapes where he breaks trail. Under the venerable sled, breakfast talk went right to the controversy over allowing oil exploration and production in the Arctic National Wildlife Refuge (ANWR). The Mackeys applauded the checks and balances that ensured environmental sensitivity during the planning and construction of the Prudhoe Bay oilfields and Trans Alaska pipeline. They thought the habituation of naive species and the evolving caution of energy giants allows them to co-exist. I muttered misgivings about putting the Arctic National Wildlife Refuge at risk for a six-month fix of crude oil for the lower 48. Clay kicked me under the table and said he was anxious to work on the truck and get on with it. He said he couldn't wait to show me the Central Arctic caribou herd.

When we changed the shattered tires, we broke two big lug wrenches. The steel snapped easily after the wrenches had been out in the cold for more than a few minutes. There are design factors that account for cold weather that are incorporated into the manufacture of rubber, metals, fuels, coffee, and humans too, for that matter. But all the design criteria for making things that are useful where people can live and work had no sway over the winter of 1989 in the Arctic. Eighty degrees below zero is ruinously cold.

By 11:00 A.M. indirect sunlight was competing with the goldish-pink glow from the parking-lot lights. The shattered tires were changed, and since he couldn't get a replacement U-joint, Clay slid under the truck and welded the loose one solid. We drove away slowly anticipating the grinding lurch that meant the Freightliner had come undone. The U-joint held. Clay shook his head repeating, "Astonishing, she's an astonishing piece of work."

The tincture of sunrise suffusing the tops of the Endicott Mountains to the west tailgated us for the next few hours. Just before we crossed a bridge at the north end of the Dietrich valley, we stopped to look at an overturned tractor and trailer load of pipe about 50 yards down from the road. "This is an unforgiving corner." Clay said, as he downshifted to a stop. He ducked into the sleeper and I climbed out his door. I wanted to photograph the scene in the soft light. I framed a few shots with wreckage foreground, pipeline midground, and Brooks Range background. When I climbed back into the cab, Clay was playing Omar and the Howlers doing "Hard Times in the Land of Plenty." He estimated that righting the wreck and towing fees to Fairbanks would cost about $14,000.

By 1:00 P.M. we were 80 miles north of Coldfoot on the Chandalar Shelf. The temperature had warmed up to 65 below zero. On that barren, high plain there is a solitary white spruce at the roadside with an official Alyeska Pipeline Company sign in front of it that reads, "Farthest North Tree on the Pipeline Corridor. Do Not Cut."

Midway through the Chandalar Shelf we came to a checkpoint. From that point on travelers must have permits. We stopped at the vacant guardhouse to stretch our legs and look around. Dozens of peaks surround the wide valley, all of them over 7,500 feet tall and nameless on maps. We were standing at the headwaters of the great Kuparuk watershed that drains into the Beaufort Sea. Clay talked about his wish to see Siberia, the Asian twin for the Alaska Arctic.

Atigun Pass loomed ahead as the valley narrowed and we rolled along next to the pipeline. The 6,800 foot pass posed one of the greatest challenges to pipeline and road construction in the entire 800 mile length of the corridor. But it is the path of least resistance through the Brooks Range, where 8,000 foot peaks rising from near sea level are the rule. The road climbed up a massive treeless side hill then turned a couple miles up and disappeared into what looked to be an impossibly steep mountain valley. Clay declared that for the next hour or so we'd be driving on the "granddaddy truck-eater of them all" and figured he had seen about 200 wrecks on Atigun Pass. A sign at the foot of the pass reads, "Avalanches Next 44 Miles."

He told me about spending three days in his sleeper when a series of three avalanches partially buried his truck a few weeks before. The first one stopped him and blocked the road, so he climbed back into his sleeper and was awakened by a second that pushed his truck towards the edge of the road. The third buried most of the cab and jammed the whole outfit against the guardrail. He dug a breather-hole for the air-cleaner canister on the side of the truck, restarted the engine, and read Larry McMurtry's Lonesome Dove for three days until help arrived. He told me, "If we spin out, try to jump out my door." If I were to jump out my side, he said, I could fall 600 feet or more. The guardrail had been replaced a couple months prior, but in the first seven or eight miles of the ascent, it had already been bent, scraped, or torn away completely.

As we climbed the pass, we emerged into the sunlight we had only seen on the peaks that enfolded the valleys we'd passed through. In the direct light the snow finally looked white. In the strained and sidelong half-light of the low valleys, the snow took on colors that transcended mere pastels. Mid-winter arctic landscapes spread out in montane fingers of lavender and magenta that cast enormous shadows of light violet. Iced riparian courses were braids of turquoise under skies that slowly turned from crimson to flesh. Clay said people wonder why Eskimos stuck here. He shrugged his shoulders and laid his palm upward as though receiving a gift through the windshield.

At the summit of Atigun Pass, Clay Gustaves exulted, "This is it, the top of my world. It's all downhill from here." The top of his world was pure white and true blue. Two ravens casually kept pace just outside our windows. "A lot of guys throw food to them," he said. Their black beaks opened and closed noiselessly. He downshifted and we descended the arctic slope of the Brooks Range to the sweeping steppes and plains that drain to Prudhoe Bay, some 150 miles north.

The vast valley of the Roche Moutons in the upper reaches of the Sagavanirktok River was as barren as any place we had seen in the 360 miles we'd come. Yet hundreds of Dall's sheep clustered in groups of twenty and thirty up there, making their living in the wind and snow in unknowable ways. One small herd, seemingly oblivious, was watched by a lone black wolf that was crouched 100 feet downwind. Clay slowed to a crawl. The wolf watched, studying the herd to see if there was a chance for an easy meal. If a wolf gets hurt at all while trying for a kill, that injury can affect the predator mortally. Insouciance forestalls oblivion for those sheep; looking and acting healthy actually prolongs life.

"In the summer it is gorgeous up here. It looks like Ireland for a couple of months," Clay stated as he worked the Freightliner back up through the gears. He added, "Walk a mile out there in August, the mosquitoes would probably kill you. In the Arctic, there's more blood lost, by far, to mosquitoes than predators."

By 2:30 P.M. the sun was behind the peaks to the west. Dall's sheep loafed on the sunlit slopes to the east. Caribou in hundreds of small herds were scattered around the million-acre Sagwon Plain, a desert landscape formed more by wind than glaciation or moving water. We could see for twenty miles in any direction, and the only things casting shadows on the snow were mammals and the Freightliner. By the time we descended Franklin's Bluffs and reached the coastal plain, we had seen thousands of Caribou, hundreds of Dall's sheep, dozens of moose, a musk ox, some Arctic foxes, and that lone wolf.

When we passed by Pump Station Two at 3:30 P.M. it was full dark and the dashboard temperature reading was 79 below zero.

Fifty-eight miles from Prudhoe Bay the road is mostly a downhill straightaway. Clay had the Freightliner in overdrive, doing 85 miles per hour. We were the only truck in the Arctic and it was just as well. Snowdrifts narrowed the road to one lane, and in places blocked it altogether. Clay aimed us down the center of the road, right at the drifts, and our 99,000 pound-live weight delivered us through them in blizzards of displaced snow that rocked the truck and obscured vision totally. But by now, help could be summoned on the C.B. radio. To slow down would only mean we'd be ignominiously mired, T-boned into a drift the size of a school bus.

From twenty miles south of Prudhoe Bay, the immensity, perhaps the enormity, of the oilfields was staggering. The view, as we descended to sea level, was of a 35-mile-long sprawl of lights that defined the 900 wells, major facilities, two airports, and countless roads. It looked like a big city. The Prudhoe Bay oilfields have cost more than 20 billion dollars to develop. They comprise the biggest oil production facility in North America. Clay turned on the radio to listen to the broadcast from Point Barrow, some 170 miles to the west of Prudhoe Bay. The announcer was speaking in Inupiaq, introducing golden oldies from the fifties.

On that last stretch of road, Clay talked about his forthcoming year off. He was going to ship his Harley to his dad's shop in Idaho and spend a month or so rebuilding it. He would paint it, "Two-Click Red." I asked him to describe that shade and he looked at me archly. "The color of those red shoes that take Dorothy home in the Wizard of Oz," he said. Once he fixes her up, Clay wants to ride the old cream puff to warm places. He thinks a year on paved roads will make him lonely for the Arctic. He told me I had just seen one of his favorite trips ever on the Haul Road. During the 23 hour trip the average temperature had been 73 below zero. He was already calling on his C.B., arranging to do what he called "hostling." He intended to drop this load, turn right back, and begin pulling those half dozen abandoned loads to their intended destinations.

I talked him into joining me at the Deadhorse Motel for supper before he went back down the road. Over Lobster Thermidor we talked of all-time engineering accomplishments like the pyramids, Hoover Dam and others. We agreed that the Haul Road and pipeline demand admiration on their own merits as unparalleled feats of engineering. Clay told me there was a monument down in Valdez to commemorate the completion of the pipeline and road. The plaque reads, "We didn't know it couldn't be done." He said that is a cliché up here anymore, but it's still the theme. Then he headed back out to his idling Freightliner for another arctic truck ride.

About a month after I returned from Alaska, news of the Exxon Valdez oil spill in Prince William Sound intruded like a blizzard on Easter weekend. I phoned a number of Alaskans I had met during my travels to hear their reactions. Feelings ran from dismay to outrage. For many workers up there life is risky, but despite long odds against them, a frontier spirit pervades and the jobs get done well and properly. Now a sense of betrayal or defeat seemed to have traumatized those I spoke with. Alaskans were mourning.

After making a few phone calls, I located Clay Gustaves in Idaho, where he was vacationing and fixing his "scooter" up for a ride to sunny climes. I wanted to know how he felt about the oil spill. "Appalling," he said, "We've been working towards a tragedy for ten years without admitting it." He slowed down, "It is the sure and final loss of innocence for Alaska." He spoke of the 900 trips he made from Fairbanks up the Pipeline Haul Road to the North Slope. He is proud of never having wrecked a truck, prouder still of never hitting or injuring a moose or caribou. Like many Alaskans engaged in dangerous tasks of extraction, whether fishing, mining, logging, or producing oil, Clay has always acted heedfully. "I loved the demands of that kind of driving, and it made me rich. I loved the risks, the excitement. I love the Arctic," he said. "It was like a jackpot just getting bigger all the time but none of us let ourselves think it could turn tragic so fast." There was a very long pause. "I won't partake again," he said. "I was only going to take a year off, but now I swear I'm not going back."

Damned Bear

(previously published in Montana Quarterly)

Author Note: Scott McMillion ran this somewhat controversial essay a few months after I wrote it, in 2012

This past summer I was within an arm's length of a black bear several times and within a couple paces of him more times than I can count. One evening, two inches, some aluminum bars, and a corncob pipe separated my face and that of a freaked out full-grown male black bear.

This bear business began with a tentative spring. As bears along the Divide emerge from hibernation, they head down stream, following their noses out of the snowfields and deep drifts in the timber at higher elevations, famished. They eat grasses and new shoots emerging at the edges of snowfields and they work their way into the low ground and river bottoms. Along the way they roll kitchen-range sized rocks aside and they dip their paws into the ants they've uncovered and lick them up. I see bear sign nearly every spring, but they're reticent, they'll run from a yapping lapdog because of their aversion to loud noises.

My surrounding neighbors are ranchers and they time the breeding of their cows so that their calves are born in February and March, often these wee creatures are born during the harshest weather we get, ice and freezing rain, and the calves that don't live are stacked in "bone piles" out towards the edge of the property. About the time the calf carcasses begin to thaw out, the bears are done hibernating and they have a dandy source of protein right where they found it last year. But the calving season was a disappointment to the post-hibernation bears hitting bone piles along the west slopes of the continental divide in Montana during the spring of 2008. The calves dropped into relatively balmy meadows and the bears were left living close to the bone.

One morning in mid May, the day after my annual Maypole party, I walked out my mud room door and found about 15 sacks of the winter's trash spread out around my new house, including some redolent remains of the Maypole party, hundreds of paper plates, disposable aluminum casserole dishes, cups, and plastic cutlery. Excuse me, but who wants to wash plastic forks?

My home, the second I've built on this 140 acre place, has about an acre of level ground around it and resides under the shade of four big ponderosa pines and a copse of cottonwoods. For more than 30 years I have put bagged trash in an old Ford pickup all winter and in the spring, when it is close to overflowing, I jumpstart it and haul the accumulated trash to the town dump. Seems efficient, just a couple trips to the dump per year suffice.

I knew immediately that this was the nocturnal doings of a bear and I lamented the fact that I have but one dog these days, a smallish, deaf 14 year old Australian shepherd that ain't much in the sight of a ravening bear. I spent a couple hours cleaning up everything from yesterday's party remains to last autumn's suspect toilet tissues, handling such grossities as paper plates replete with congealed fat, rotten green salad and beer cups with what I believed to be bear tooth marks. Chewed and rejected lumps of tinfoil kept catching my eye. I didn't know bears regurgitated anything and I felt they might be more fastidious than I'd ever figured.

As I was resacking the trash, picking up what looked like vomited bits of plastic forks and other remnants, I came across a sodden little brown flannel purse. Tucked in the purse were a film can half full of reefer and a miniature corncob pipe. I stuck the dope in my freezer, a tacit disavowal of this contraband, even though, at the time I had a marijuana card prescribed by a Helena doctor. This new breed of dope is too much for my old lungs. Then I gassed up and jumpstarted the old Ford, and made the dump run.

When I got back there was a message on my phone from a neighbor telling me to watch out for this bear that's around because it was not showing any fear of humans or dogs. It had broken into the neighbor's hen house and eaten all the chicken feed. I imagined shelves full of roosting hens terrified, watching this huge intruder having his way with their coop.

That night I awoke to my dog Max barking out on the kitchen deck.

Bears are timid creatures until hunger overcomes shyness. With but one old dog barking at him there was nothing much to deter his quest for the next meal. For 30 years I've left a metal trashcan with a fist-sized hole in the bottom, full of dog food just outside the door under the porch roof. The dogs have always just helped themselves and they never get fat because I buy dog food they don't seem to care for. They have a geothermally heated doghouse that they share with the cats, which are fed similarly, out of open bags of cat chow left in a couple places accessible only by cat. This setup allows me to leave for a week or two, and throughout the years it has served the critters and me well. I've always had three dogs at a time and a pack like that, working in concert, will chase a bear away. I lost my dog, Ernie, last winter. Like a few others, he just disappeared. Then old Lucky's luck ran out at 15, and I was down to one pretty somnolent dog. I've lost dogs and cats, over the years, to mountain lions, foxes, coyotes and wolves, but the timidity of bears has kept them from hanging around until I got down to old Max, who appeared to have reached an understanding with this pig of a bear. This bear would ignore my dog while gorging on that mutt's gravy train.

I tramped upstairs and out the mudroom door and there, in my myopia and the scrim of moonlight, was a full-grown black bear hunched over and feeding at the trashcan of dry dog food while old Max yapped. I could have touched the bear. He looked over his massive, seemingly boneless shoulder and I wondered if he was going to fight me for the food.

The conventional wisdom when suffering a bear attack goes something like this: A grizzly will attack a human because it is protecting something; a food cache, or their offspring. The grizzly wants you to submit, one should curl up in a fetal position with your arms wrapped around your head, and then most of the time, after inflicting pretty serious damage on the arms and head, the grizzly figures it has prevailed and leaves the scene. Do not fight back with a grizzly; you'll only prolong the attack. When attacked by a black bear, on the other hand, one should fight back as though your life depends upon winning because black bears attack humans out of hunger and a little desperation, they intend to kill you and eat you and unless it occurs to the bear that this is way too difficult as you gouge eyes, kick, slug, pummel, they will make a meal of you. Further complicating this scenario, however, is the fact there are wildlife biologists who have survived bear attacks who, at the moment they were jumped, could not identify which species was ripping into them. They report curling up and protecting their heads, and fortunately, that mollified what was probably a grizzly.

My usual contingent of three dogs have always defended this cache from any and all bears, rats, foxes, coyotes, raccoons and birds. This bear's disregard for lonely old Max represented a disconcerting boldness. I hollered something unintelligible even to me and he lumbered away, his undulating blackness rolling deliberately, his ears cocked back. I choked off gratuitous curses as they sprang to mind, why, I don't know. I brought Max inside wondering how a dog and a bear could be that close and nothing bigger happened. Ineffectual as Max had been, he stuck.

Before breakfast I brought the dog food can inside the mudroom. I also stashed the greasy little barbecue in the guest house, but I have a big one I made from a 300 gallon fuel tank that is as unwieldy as an upright piano, and it is laden with greasy ashes and, as far as I'm concerned, immovable. To eliminate any attraction for bears I'd essentially have to quit living here and raising food and hosting large parties where I commonly feed more than 100 humans. The compost piles at the greenhouse and garden are redolent and must smell like a smorgasbord to an omnivore. To eliminate all bear attractants I'd have to quit barbecuing and probably wash down any spots outdoors where juice or beer spilled. We'd have to eschew the raw oyster feed at the annual Thanksgiving party and haul away the midden that has grown beside the office deck for 25 years. In short, I'd pretty much have to close the place and move. There, unfortunately, is no compromising with a bear that owns a memory of a food source. I thought of my bear as a rat. I was trying to figure out, essentially, what to do with a rat. I learned that bears are a lot more heart-rending than any rat.

That night I awoke to scratching and thumping noises up around the mudroom and when I hollered "goddamit" out my basement bedroom window the demolition sounds paused briefly, and started in again. I got my 20 gauge and walked out the basement door and pumped a couple rounds into the air and once my ears quit ringing things seemed to have quieted down. I felt weary of encounters with a large predator in the middle of the night.

The next morning I found four batten boards on my mudroom had been pried off and deep claw marks on the adjacent boards that, fortunately, I had screwed down. I've heard several stories of bears tearing through cheap siding, insulation, and sheetrock and completely wrecking kitchens. This bear had developed a dangerous craving and was attempting to break into my home, sensing the dog food stash through the board and batten siding and lord knows what other compelling scents.

I called Fish and Game and later that day the game warden from nearby Missoula hauled in a bear trap that completely occupied his pickup bed. It was a six-sided contraption, like a huge, crude barrel eight feet long, about four feet wide and five feet tall. At one end, above an opening that you could roll a truck tire through, a trapdoor loomed like a guillotine. It looked shiny and angular and otherworldly, like something the space shuttle might deploy. The warden told me it was brand new. I thought, "untested."

We wrestled and skidded it until it was angled out of the pickup and one end rested on the ground. Then he pulled the pickup forward, driving out from under it real fast, presumably so it wouldn't tear off his back bumper when it fell out the rest of the way. It wasn't on level ground and I could make it rock a little.

"Set the door right, and when it slams down this thing will hold a full grown griz," the warden said. He patted the trap, and added, "Too bad we couldn't get her leveled off better. Well, I bet it stays shut."

He looked beleaguered, and was. He told me there were more bears out getting in trouble this year than he could remember. He figured it was the short bone piles and the tentative spring that was offering more snow than we'd had through the winter and the paucity of fresh, green shoots.

He showed me how to bait and set the trap and advised me to put my dog and cats indoors before I set it.

The way it works is that the bear smells the bait at the far end of the trap and enters through the open trap door. When the bear paws at the burlap sack with the fish in it at the far end a cord from the sack pulls a lever and the trap door slams down and locks in place. The door was nearly too heavy for one guy, he said, and he asked me to try to lift it. I could, and then I let it down slowly.

That evening my daughter, Flannery, and I were working in the greenhouse and by about 7 o'clock she wanted to drive back to Helena, while it was still light out. Once she and her rangy pit bull cross left, I sequestered my cats and Max and baited the burlap sack with a can of salmon, and as the warden had advised, I poured a can of Coca Cola over everything and at the entrance, and set the trap door.

I walked back up to my office, a two minute stroll, about 800 feet, and just as I got there I heard a loud glang and some moaning and roaring and thumping noises. That bear must have been watching me and then went directly to the odor of the Coke and fish when I'd cleared out. I heard a metallic thumping and more outraged roars and went down to the trap, which was about 50 feet from my kitchen door. The bear was in there crashing from one end to the other slapping at the doors and biting at the bars over the 10 inch square opening through which a roiling blackness with tan flews and big white teeth appeared. With his teeth caught on the bars he emitted a heartbreaking three-note lament that sounded like a jeremiad to panic and fear. This powerful, unfettered creature was now caged; his wretched sobs and claustrophobic crashing around told me he knew he was damned.

Bears are willing entrants into tight, dark places, they den up and hibernate, they find food under logs and rocks and their claws are perfectly evolved digging tools. He'd followed the extravagant scent of canned salmon and Coke and then, when he tugged at the redolent sack he heard the loudest noise he'd ever experienced a couple feet behind him and he was confined. Caves, tunnels, dugouts, mean security to bears. This construct, this slope-sided metal chamber that he couldn't dig a claw into captured his entirety. The kind of space that always offered cozy sanctuary was now his prison.

He kept smashing himself around in there, poking his claws through the air holes at the top and biting at the bars on the tiny windows at each end and his moans would ascend and descend that heart rending three-note scale. There was blood around every one of the 1 inch air holes across the top of the trap, his claws were getting stuck and the pads of his feet, or roots of his claws were torn. He charged the little barred windows and tore at the air holes above him for all he was worth. His worth, his life roaming free under the sky had never been constrained, had never been taken away. The stench of shit, piss, anguish, and fear were thick enough to smell from my kitchen door. He seemed to know he was fighting for his life and I could imagine this battle inside the dark trap going on until he died in there. The easy life, feeding at the dog food can had habituated and undone him.

I phoned the game warden and he said he couldn't come and pick up the trap and bear until about 10:00 the next morning, so I had this accursed beast to deal with and it sounded like he would be keening and clanking out there all night, further injuring himself in his incessant frenzy to be free. The blood around the air holes and on the bars of the little windows was most troubling and building up. I wished I had a tranquilizer gun, or at least some Valium I could feed him in hamburger, anything to calm him down.

Then I remembered the pot in my freezer. I loaded up the little corncob pipe and sat at the end of the trap where the bait had hung. The 10 inch square window with the welded bars on it didn't allow much of a view in there, but I packed and lit the pipe in a breeze and blew some smoke towards the bars. I remembered an interview I'd done on a story about smokejumpers and how they'd told me that sometimes, when they'd jumped fairly young fires that were just catching some midday wind that shifted suddenly, they'd run from the wind-driven flames and occasionally they'd be in a foot race that included the local wildlife fleeing too. One guy, Wayne Williams, said he'd run alongside bears and elk and rabbits and all manner of mammals. So smoke would be nothing new to this bear, I reasoned.

The breeze that washed over the scene carried most of the smoke away so I took another drag and got my face about two inches from the window. My bear smashed his muzzle against the bars, uttering a groan that sounded infuriated. Droplets of spittle pelted my face. His teeth gnashed and clicked against the bars. Pretty strange apparition to behold at the end of the pot pipe you're smoking, but I was determined to sedate him and the welds in aluminum bars looked respectable. I sat there and loaded the pipe up again and redoubled my efforts and blew more smoke in there with him. By the third pipe full, probably about fifteen big puffs of smoke moving through the trap and out the bloody air holes on top, that bear was sitting about a foot from the trap's window, becalmed. Bears, apparently, have cannabanoid receptors just like humans. Maybe he'd gotten used to my face at the window and cut his losses on the big, bad bear act, but I figured he must have been about as zonked as I was. I felt redeemed, but responsible; host like.

I went back into my kitchen and retrieved a couple pounds of shrimp I'd cooked the night before, when expected company didn't show up. I took some salad tongs, and figuring the bear had the munchies too, I went out and dropped a few between the bars, which he loudly lapped up. Then he accepted a few dozen more right from the tongs. I considered feeding him from my fingers, just like we did with cherry Lifesavers to two black bears out of the windows of the 1958 Chevy station wagon in Yellowstone Park, when I was an impressionable nine year old. Call it nostalgia. We finished the shrimp. Then I suddenly wondered if I'd just committed some offense against nature or if this had been a forgivable humanitarian impulse.

I called a friend, a highly placed official in the Montana Department of Fish, Wildlife and Parks, and confessed. He wishes to conceal his identity for obvious reasons, but he said "Don't quote me, but if medical marijuana helps humans, as the voters of Montana have so wisely mandated, who are we to deny it to our cousins?" More comfortable with my decision, I went back out to get the bear restoned before bed.

I arose at dawn and went out to the bear trap and rigged a cheap blue tarp over the cage so it wouldn't get too hot in there under the rising sun. My bear buddy made a few more laments in there and then started in again, tearing at the air holes so I retrieved the dope and sat by the window and he sat there grunting but didn't try to bite his way through the bars, just pressed his cue ball sized nose against them. I shared a bowl with him; one for the road, so to speak.

About 10 A.M. a couple of game wardens showed up with a winch and ramp equipped truck and appreciated my effort to shade the beast. The alpha warden treated his somewhat bear-shaped, loutish assistant with open disdain, especially when he spoke into his shirt collar, like a television cop. "This bear is way too habituated," the boss said. "Bad sign that he's so calm around us." I agreed. Unfortunately that was too true.

They phoned later and said they'd dropped him off about fifty miles away, up near the ghost town of Garnet. They'd "doped" him and installed a green ear tag, they explained. Should he show up anywhere around humans he'd have to be put down. I wondered why green.

About a week later I was at my kitchen sink doing dishes and I could feel the kitchen wall shudder. The window above the sink overlooks the deck and there was my bear with his green ear tag dully visible in the light from the house. He sat on my deck without acknowledging me, like he was just glad to be back. I sneaked downstairs and got my 20 gauge and crept back up the stairs, burst out the mudroom door, and screamed "GODDAMIT" as loudly as I could and he took off running and I let him get about thirty-five yards away and peppered his ass with No. 8 birdshot. Aversion therapy is cruel by definition and I prayed he'd associate this place with fright and a pain in the ass.

The next morning the talk at the Avon café, the gossip mill, as I regard it, was that late the night before a beekeeper watched through the night vision scope on his 30/30, a bear wrecking his hives. He fired and figured he must have wounded the critter, he said he lost sight of the bear.

The damned bear ran out on highway 12, right in front of a semi and probably died instantly, and the trucker didn't even slow down.

I kept quiet and couldn't finish my omelet and thought about sharing shrimp with a sentient being I'd medicated, wondering how I might have changed this outcome, knowing that was foolish, but just as the bear had followed his nose into a small, seemingly safe place, I'd been unwittingly trapped too.

Black Ice

(previously published in Northern Lights, Winter 1994)

Author Note: This is a composite essay built from a couple of my experiences as an EMT in western Montana.

"I ain't bettin' the ranch that I'll never catch AIDS doing this," Dan said, and after he'd said it a few times he quit answering the calls. Wally never said a thing, he just quit coming to training sessions until his rating lapsed. For years we'd tacitly acknowledged that we were fools playing a thankless and dangerous game. I was the holdout, voluntarily responding to car wrecks and medical emergencies, and then living with the recurring vignettes of trauma and death. This evening it was Mutt's turn.

I'd never seen Mutt without a hat and here he was, bald. Furrows of blanched skin ascended to the top of his cranium, parallel to his silver, untamed eyebrows as though he were still surprised. He was toothless, naked and lifeless; eyes opaque as the sky-blue bathroom floor, pupils fixed and dilated. He must have been shaving; the lather on his cheeks had dried to the look of angel food cake. He'd been shaving before bedtime, which struck me as romantic.

It had taken me about twenty minutes of driving on snow packed and icy roads to get to the ranch after the screaming, sobbing phone call from Lily, his wizened wife of 40 years. At least I didn't have to worry about catching AIDS on this response. Not from old Mutt.

Every time I answered one of those beseeching calls, whether it was a medical emergency, or one of those god-awful head-ons from highway 12, I wondered how long it would be until I ended up HIV positive, or with that Hepatitis C that nothing could fix. It was an issue at home that we tiptoed around. My wife knew intuitively that I couldn't stop going out to help folks who were suddenly in the biggest trouble of their lives. "You're doing good work. There's no money involved. I don't think the universe will punish you for that," she said, unconvincingly.

I figured I'd probably get infected working on some carload of baked kids heading home from Missoula's bar scene to the sanctimony of Helena. Several times I'd found drug paraphernalia and empty beer bottles at single vehicle wrecks where no one survived and I stomped the evidence into a snow bank before the highway patrol arrived, thinking that these folks' families had enough to go through. Ice, gravity and delusions of total control can undo the best of us, thus we see single vehicle wrecks.

As a volunteer, trained E.M.T., I always work on trying to be as compassionate as possible with the folks I help. In western Montana empathy goes mostly unrecognized and sympathy redounds more commonly to doctoring dumb animals. Working on unconscious humans is a lot like practicing veterinary medicine and offers plenty of room for kindheartedness without getting all tangled up in pathos, which would be going over the line. I was terribly aware that panic or despair could overwhelm me at the moment when people needed exacting emergency medical procedures. When faced with someone who may well die unless you do everything right, you fall back on protocols and checklists, and you may forget to be compassionate while distracted by your own fear, your revulsion.

Among other emergency medical procedures, I'd delivered two babies, grateful for the ease of my part while the young mothers, homebound by drifting snow, had worked harder at pushing those babies out than any muscular feat I had ever seen. The fathers, absorbed and awash in the sweaty drama, naturally abandoned pretenses of modesty. Attending births was one part of emergency care that gave me few misgivings. Having delivered our two kids, I was tooled up with a Doppler monitor for listening to fetal heart tones during contractions. I had oxygen masks sized for newborns. I knew how to do an episiotomy, but dreaded that eventuality.

Most of the calls for help came from car wrecks that occurred in the wee hours after the bars closed. We averaged 17 highway wreck responses per year. On our narrow, two lane mountain roads, when vehicles collided, I often had to hacksaw my way into upside down cars or break out windows only to find that the folks were dead. Otherwise, I had to "package" and extract the unconscious, without compromising their spinal cords. Imagine a physician who must saw and crowbar his way into a wrecked car to begin stabilizing you, and you begin to understand this E.M.T. work. I usually skinned a knuckle or cut my hands doing vehicle extractions. I was always aware that my blood and theirs got mixed.

A few times, when I'd responded to a wreck, I'd go home and just burn my clothes, even the 100 dollar insulated coveralls I wore in the winter. The fabric got so blood-soaked and stained with every kind of body fluid that there was to be no soapy redemption for my clothing. No avoiding or discounting the gore, with the attendant reminders that stained my clothing and my senses. You can taste copper for a week or more after you do C.P.R. on someone who was bleeding from the mouth when they quit breathing. One-percent of the time that you do C.P.R it works. I'd done C.P.R. four times on old friends and hapless strangers. It had never worked. For months afterward I didn't believe that I would ever want to try it again.

I had my elbows locked. From my knees I pushed down hard on Mutt's sternum—counting the compressions out loud—then I pinched his wide nose shut, straightened and stretched his neck, and blew a few breaths into his mouth. His nose hairs tickled against my face. The verbal cadence of the chest compressions and the blowing noises I made ventilating Mutt's corpse kept the family from coming into the bathroom. I knew they could hear me in there working away on him. I do C.P.R noisily, just so the family knows that everything was tried. You don't do C.P.R. unless someone's breathing and pulse have stopped, so you are always doing it, clinically speaking, on a cadaver. I do it loudly for the family and I try to keep it up for as long as I can so that they have time to begin to understand that everything is changing.

I kept pumping his chest and blowing in his rubbery mouth, sweating on him and feeling the burn in my arms and shoulders. Twice, as I compressed his chest, I heard the soft pop of Mutt's ribs breaking. That's a part of C.P.R. that makes me wince when I think about this stuff afterwards. There's also a problem with gastric distension, when too much air goes into the abdomen via the esophagus. The thing to do then is roll their head to the side and pump out the air; the stomach contents come out with it, lubricating their mouth which makes it much more difficult to get a good seal when you clamp your mouth on theirs to breathe into them.

Mutt's whiskers gave me purchase on his slippery old lips.

His kids and grandkids were arriving out in the kitchen, scraping chairs and clomping around in cowboy boots. A few phrases and loud words strained through the wall into the bathroom: "He bought that for me," and, "Like hell they will." A chair rasped across the floor, and over that racket someone said, "Don't ever talk water rights with anybody." Another voice, raising the decibels, said, "He was not." I hated hearing the past tense used on Mutt.

I could hear Lily in the living room with a few murmuring daughters-in-law but she sounded alone, "Ninety bred heifers," she moaned, "what'm I supposed to do?"

I kept up the C.P.R. from training, and to protect myself from the family mess brewing out there. My people hug and cry and we use whiskey in our coffee in these deals and we try to go easy on each other.

During the past fifteen years I'd helped Mutt out for a few days every spring, usually riding his two-cylinder John Deere "D" tractor pulling a wishbone harrow through his worn out alfalfa fields. I liked to stand when I steered that tractor. Once, in a riverside meadow where cottonwoods and willows buffered Lump gulch, there was a nest of ground wasps that I stirred up on each pass. Those wasps ganged up and attacked and wasted themselves stinging the vertical exhaust pipe about five feet in front of my face, but they never tried a thing on me. I felt as invulnerable standing on that tractor as a skipper cruising coastal waters and I laughed out loud at the obstinacy of wasps every time I plowed through their swarms. Mutt chugged across the meadow on his 9N Ford tractor. I had stopped, just daring those wasps to come, but they were convinced that the exhaust pipe was the enemy. Mutt's voice carried over our idling tractors and he said there must be a high-pressure system, that the dense air was carrying sounds. He'd heard me laughing from the next field, on the other side of the windrowed willows, where he was disking.

He watched the wasps dropping from the hot exhaust pipe to the engine cowling like popcorn and said, "Interesting life, if you're crazy, or just willing." I didn't know if he meant the wasps or me. He laughed, wheeled around, and said, "No fraternizing with the help." He dropped his tool bar and cultivated his own tracks, leaving his cross-purposes through my designs in the dirt.

A couple of weeks ago Mutt had phoned and asked me to come and see something special. I drove up that night; my headlights swept the subtle swells of his snow-dressed hayfields and settled on his twelve foot tall shop door. Inside, under the rafters of the cavernous cinder block shop he'd finished installing what he called his "traveling bridge crane," a series of I-beams and rolling winches that he'd bolted and welded up there like the framework of a skyscraper.

"I can lift five tons thirteen foot in the air anywhere in this building and set it down anywhere else in here," he crowed, as he walked around tilting his eyes and stretching his neck towards the apparatus.

He had attached four chains around the axles of the 9N Ford which he lifted off the old Chevy flatbed that creaked up under the rising weight a good five inches. His forearms were as thick as a bear's and he carefully worked the three buttons on the hanging electric switch in one grime-lined paw.

He laid his free arm across my chest and backed me out from under the tractor.

"Never trust a skyhook," he said.

"I trust your welds, Mutt," I told him.

Mutt smiled up at the cruciform chassis of the tractor moving sedately under the fluorescent lights.

"Look Ma, one hand," he chuckled, as the tractor descended towards an empty space in the center aisle.

"Real back saver," he said, "real body saver."

"You got it made now, Mutt," I said, thinking that the bridge crane really would save him. "You're gonna be looking for things to pick up."

The last thing he picked up was a plastic razor.

Martin, the eldest son, stepped into the bathroom. He said, "The ambulance is on the way. Doctor Peavy said to discontinue C.P.R.," like he was telling me not to pet his dog. "Why the hell did you do it at all, Harp? You know he didn't want to be a vegetable." His cowboy boots looked as shiny as black ice. "I said why'd you do it, Harp? Goddamnit." Marty stomped his foot and some fluids from his dad slopped up onto his boot.

I was still bent over Mutt. My arms ached. My florid hands were splayed on his pallid, grizzled chest. I didn't want to look above the ironed crease in Marty's jeans. I didn't want to take my hands off Mutt. I didn't want to stand up because I'm six foot two and my dislike for the alpha male crap makes me go kind of hunchbacked and inarticulate in confrontations. I rocked back on my heels to see Marty's face. My mouth and beard were as slimed as his dad's. He looked at my face, then at Mutt's, and then covered his mouth with both hands.

"Had to Marty," I said, "Lily called me and I came and did what I learned to do." I tasted old Mutt, looked down at him and swallowed. "I wasn't trying to drag everything out. I guess I'm just trying to help."

"Are you done?" Marty sniffed.

"Mutt," I blurted, "is a remarkable character."

Marty left. His boots and the door both echoed shortly in the tiled bathroom.

I looked Mutt over and believed that he really was dead then.

No more fun in the meadows and the shop.

I thought about Doctor Peavy seeing Mutt's belly swollen with air when he saw him in the Deer Lodge E.R. and pronounced him D.O.A. The doc would chew my butt for not following the protocol. I rolled his head to one side and pumped hard on his abdomen a couple times and cried a little. Air wheezed out of his body for the last time. I covered Mutt and the mess with some bath towels and washed up over the bathtub so I wouldn't have to straddle him where he was shrouded under the sink. Then I stole his blue plastic razor. I put it in my shirt pocket, wanting to save a few tiny hairs for an amulet that would safeguard his memory.

The family members in the kitchen went stiff and silent when I emerged from the bathroom. The burnt coffee smell seemed to compete with the stench of years of family shit piling up around the table. "Sorry for your troubles," I said, hunched over and working the Velcro closure of my jump kit. I slipped through the tension and left like a cat. My dirty Ford pickup windows were frosted up under a puny yard light.

The drive home, down the slalom curves of Blackfoot canyon, unfolded slowly. The snow, plowed and piled on the road's edge, had thawed that afternoon and water had flowed across the pavement and frozen into patches of black ice. The defroster hadn't made it to the edges of the windshield. Snow layered up the canyon walls doubled the glow of the crescent moon and the starlight filtered in from the Milky Way.

My thoughts were as dark and cold as the insides of my gloves. I gripped the steering wheel too hard on an icy patch in the horseshoe curve, the back end broke out and slid, and I took too long to recover control. I forced myself to slow down. "Just trying to help," I told myself over and over, "why bother?" I had picked the place where I was making a place for my family, I thought, but I sure as hell couldn't pick whomever else I helped.

Being the volunteer paramedic, where the nearest hospital is fifty miles away, sometimes seemed as marginalized as being a Peace Corps volunteer on an island where I don't know the language or customs of death. Simple compassion seems of little value to people newly arrived at the scene where a family member has died. Contorted faces crumple into immediate denial followed quickly by blame or self-recriminations or down-on-your-knees prayer.

Images of death, of attending deaths, have a life of their own and a death of their own. "Give it time," I believe. But every time I played my role in an untimely death, some local talk, I was told, got around to my "hero complex." I wondered if they were right, I couldn't seem to stop responding to the calls for help, but I resented the risk I was taking and all of the unspeakable memories of people who had died with my hands on them over the years. There are always a few folks in any small town who apply a certain meanness to anything that occurs outside of their self-referencing world. I'd started doing this because of the treacherous stretch of two-lane highway through our county, from the Interstate exchange to the top of the continental Divide: 22 miles of highway that averaged 17 wrecks a year. We volunteer firefighters would take the fire truck to the accident scene with all the lights aswirl but we'd just stand around holding flashlights and directing traffic while listening to people weeping or wailing hysterically for help, trapped in their cars in the ditches. Sometimes those scenes were quiet. Wally and Dan and I had taken hundreds of hours of training and geared up out of our pockets to acquire the tools we used to help people who were sick or injured, and now with the other guys out, I was compelled to respond to people in need. There will always be some folks who find fault. I hoped to just ignore the critics or to finally understand why I kept this up.

"The thankless part is worse than the bloody part," I kept thinking as I headed home. "I'll see Lily and the boys at the funeral," I thought, "and at the post office once in a while, and we'll all spare each other any depth of feeling."

Just around the blind corner at Dooley creek there was a scene in my headlights that took some leaning and squinting to sort out. I glimpsed in passing what appeared to be a dead deer lying in front of a small car and a guy sitting on the hood with his head in his hands. I stopped and backed up close to the critter. I curled my toes and walked up the icy road flashlighting to see if the guy on the car was hurt. The motor was idling. He had his knees drawn up under him. He kept his head on his knees even though he must have heard me walk up. I was whistling the "Goddamn them all ..." chorus of "Barrett's Privateers," and trying to stay composed.

"I'm a paramedic. Can I help you?" I asked the figure on the car.

"Slipped on ice, hit my head. I think I'm okay," he said, down at his knees. "The, uh, cougar hasn't kicked for awhile."

Spotlighted in the single headlight, a dirty-looking mountain lion was sprawled on the ice, still twitching. I stepped back reflexively. Sitting just above the source of light, the man vomited between his skinny knees, onto his front bumper.

He was weeping. His high-top red tennis shoes drew my eyes like ice skates would in the summer. I offered him my coat. He accepted it. As he pulled my sleeve up his arm he pointed shakily at the road kill. He coughed at length, then blubbered in an east coast accent: "I couldn't stop. He just stood there looking at me. I only moved here this week. It was awful. My god, it's all so horrid...."

The effeminate urgency of his voice scared me. I wondered if he might be HIV positive and how I could protect myself from him. A trickle of dried blood had congealed on his forehead. His mouth was bloody. Then a little rope of pink drool whipped at his cheek when he swung his head as the lion screamed. The lion pawed at his mouth a few times as the scream receded to a wet cough.

A lot of people in Montana carry handguns in their cars. I should, I thought, as the lion convulsed on the ice.

I edged over to the cut bank that rose up the mountainside and kicked loose a pointy rock that was nearly too heavy for me to lift. Working with the bad footing, I lugged it back to the lion. It was a young male; his tawny head was more basketball-shaped than the heart shape that females conform to. He had a gash down his side. One hind leg was bent impossibly. I raised the rock chest-high and dropped it on his head. I could feel it hit him in my feet.

I sort of skated back to my pickup through the plume of exhaust, leaned into the warm cab and pulled on some latex gloves and took out some alcohol swabs. The guy was now breathing deeply and cussing quietly, a good sign, I hoped, as I approached him. I put some swabs in his bare hand and told him he ought to clean himself up.

"Do something for yourself," I said, thinking that this guy might be better off focusing on himself and because I didn't want to get mixed up with his blood and slobber.

"I'll get the cat off the road," I said, as I kicked gingerly at the lion's hindquarters. Nothing. The rock had rolled right next to his head. I couldn't lift it now, so I skidded it off the road. I kicked at the tufted pads on the lion's back legs, still ready to scramble. Dead.

"You shouldn't touch the evidence until the police come. I think wildlife is government property," came the guy's voice from above the headlight.

"There won't be any cops," I said, "Gotta clear the road."

I swung the lion around but his thick forelegs were as stout as a pint glass. I worked my bare hands into the icy fur between his pads and got a grip. Once his hair wasn't getting pulled against the grain, he slid fluidly into the ditch. His ruined head lolled and thumped against the crusty berm of plowed snow. I bent over in the verge of light and tugged at his whiskers, revealing his fangs. Holding on, I pulled a seam ripper from my shirt pocket, a tool I use for cutting away people's clothing to expose injuries, and I worked at his long whiskers until I had cut them all off and his lip dropped. His whiskers were as thick as angel hair pasta and springy. I rolled them in my fingers and tucked them into my shirt pocket with Mutt's razor thinking that they would serve as some kind of charm or amulet. Cats have whiskers to give them an extra sense of where they are, and some say, to give them better balance. Mutt's bewhiskered lips were more firm than this lion's; human speech, kissing, whistling, sucking, give our lip muscles more integrity than a lion's which are mostly there to keep the flies out or curl back to chow down. I thought that I'd rather give this lion C.P.R. than the guy on the car and I recalled a line from a Russian proverb: "Kissing a tiger is all risk and no pleasure."

I hoped all these ruminations would eventually coalesce into a sense of the evening's events. I wondered if some sort of eulogy might be appropriate. "Lionizing the lion," I thought, "to what end?" I spat in my hand and rubbed it on his clipped muzzle, smoothing it back towards his eyes, as his momma would have. "Hard luck, pal," I said out loud, "the universe punched your ticket the same day as Mutt's." That cat wasn't bucking the odds, it was just his turn. I thought about how

I'd been almost as frightened of the unwitting killer as I was of this lion, and I knew that when my number was up no amount of fear or contrived avoidance would stall my fate. Mutt had been talking to me in his alfalfa field: willingness is the big deal. Then I raked snow off the hillside onto that lion like a cat hiding scat.

The guy's head wound was too small to suture, and it had quit bleeding. He was wiping his mouth off with the alcohol swabs. I handed him my hanky, it was clean and still folded. I told him that the nearest phone would be at Eve's place, we could drive there and if he still wanted to, he could call the sheriff.

"You know," I said, "cars kill quite a few lions every winter. It's no crime. Take it easy on yourself, bub."

"My name is Richard," he said primly, "I should at least report it." He slid off the hood and looked at his car. The headlight exposed his skinny torso like a clapper in the bell of my unzipped coat. He shrugged. "I only have one headlight working."

"We'll take it easy."

"I really need some help here," he said miserably.

"Okay, Richard, follow me. We'll take her slow."

It was all downhill to the east side of Nimrod and Eve's Mountain Palace. There was enough moon and starlight to see the color of the thin, green steel fence posts forty feet from the road where the canyon opened into meadows.

"Dance On Our Walls Nightly," the sign blinked in her empty parking lot. Eve's "palace" was a twelve foot wide, double long trailer, in which, it was said, you could hit everyone in the place with one shotgun round through the bay window. A few years back a Butte carpet layer who had fallen hard for Eve had carpeted the whole place, the floor, then the walls, in a patchwork of remnants. The support posts were carpeted. The guy had started carpeting the table legs and barstools when Eve broke things off. Over the years the various rugs had become mostly stained up to shoulder level to the color of oil-soaked earth, the predominant color and odor of the loggers, miners, and ranchers who drank there.

I asked her for a couple of shots of Irish whiskey.

"Sorry, I've nothing but this Protestant shite," she said, brandishing a bottle of Bushmill's and faking an Irish accent.

"Bourbon, then," I said. "And one for this survivor, please." I pointed at Richard with my elbow. "He just took on a lion and came out on top. Let's drink to subduing the earth." I explained to Eve how Richard and I met.

Eve raised a bottle from the well and tipped it over three shot glasses. I teased her about where she could find some exotic stew fixings. "Fresh lion," I said, "think of it."

"Go to hell, Harp," she said as I tipped my shot back.

Richard said, "Phone, ma'am?"

He had slowed his speech and sort of drawled "ma'am," which made him seem less self-absorbed than I had judged him.

She held her long bare arm out and pointed towards the phone like a ballerina. "Phone, honey," she said, "911 is free." She draped a dry towel that was about the color of her platinum hair over her shoulder and rubbed her belly under her Houston Rockets jersey. Eve still looked skinny and willing. She retained the best remnants of a forty year old who'd always overdone everything. She sponsored and played third base on the local women's softball team, her throws to first were unerring and her banter sparked her teammates and kept the crowd wound up.

There's a heart-shaped birthmark on the bottom side of her left breast. If you broached the subject and caught her in the right mood she'd give you a look. She'd lift her shirt and then raise her breast up by the nipple, leaving most guys unable to watch everything to their satisfaction. She'd hold her breast by its erect nipple for a bit, and then let it rest and slide her shirt back down. Sometimes she'd surprise some guy and, unsolicited, just give him a look out of the goodness of her two hearts.

"Just heard about old Mutt," she said, "that sucks." She laid her hand on mine and said, "The way you help out...well, it means more than you know." She paused and I ached to hear more. "Knowing you're around Harp, and that you'll help—well."

I cleared my throat. "Thanks, Eve. I'll keep trying, anyway."

Richard came back from the phone, tugging at his chin whiskers. He sipped at the bourbon, then threw it back and thumped his chest lightly, a quirky gesture of the infrequent whiskey drinker that I'd bet he learned from his father.

"They don't care, as long as it's off the road. They said I could drive to Deer Lodge and fill out a form, but it'd be a waste of time. A mountain lion is dead out there," he paused and covered his mouth for a little burp, "and nobody cares."

"We don't deal with some things as well as we might around here, Richard," I said.

I told him that the lion was probably a juvenile, a coming two year old who had been run off by his mom, who'd come into estrous and was waiting for the next rutting male who would just try to kill the kid anyway.

"Whoa," Eve said sadly, "Ain't no shit like family shit."

I slid my coat off the bar. My damp hankie was stuffed in one sleeve; it fell between Richard's feet. Richard bent and picked it up and held it to me apologetically. It was bloodied along one edge and snotty. I hesitated to touch it, then I wondered how I'd come to be such a nervous white boy, and when I'd get better. I took the lion whiskers out of my chest pocket and folded them in the hanky with Mutt's razor and put the clump of fabric under my hat. I parted Richard's hair for a last check of his forehead cut and told him it was nothing to worry about, that it was crusted over already and that when the wind parted his hair he'd have a rakish little scar. Eve volunteered a Band-Aid and some "assburn."

Richard, somewhat discomposed, fished in his pocket and said, "Three whiskies, please Eve." Eve raised her green eyes to me, smiled, and poured two shots. She set four aspirins on a square Budweiser napkin.

"Four, like, with the whiskey?" he asked Eve.

"You need it, you might as well take a few," she said, shrugging.

I told Richard that if he tried to drive and lost that other headlight, he'd be stuck and cold and truly in trouble.

"My car's broken. I don't know what's next," he said, and god love him, he cast an appraising eye at Eve.

She was casually, but elegantly, wringing out a bar rag. "I like your accent, Richard. All the 'rangutans I get in here sound the same. What do you do?"

"I'm a piano tuner," he said, "a piano tuner."

"The hell," she said, wiping her hand off on her baby blue jersey, "I bet you're a good one, even if you're a scarred up old lion killer."

Richard smiled and gently palpated his little laceration. Then he picked the pills up with the tips of his slender fingers. He threw his head back like he was going to sing, dropped the aspirin in his mouth and gulped some whiskey. His Adam's apple jumped up under his jaw twice.

"Holy smokes," he said, and patted his chest again.

Eve tilted her whiskey back and refilled their shot glasses without seeming to take her eyes off him.

"Thanks, Eve," I said, as I shouldered the carpeted door.

"Keep the shiny side up," she said cheerfully.

"Good night," they said.

Richard added, "Thank you very much."

Falling Out of the Cold War

(previously published in Smithsonian Air & Space)

Author Note: This was the first of twenty-two features I wrote for Smithsonian Air & Space magazine.

"To know a thing you have to trust what you know, and all that you know, and as far as you know in whatever direction your knowing drags you." — Ken Kesey, *Sometimes a Great Notion*

My first exposure to skydiving was with Irina Solovyova, a former Soviet cosmonaut. She was in San Francisco enroute to an 800 mile ski expedition in Antarctica. Her hosts, upon learning that she was also a world champion skydiver, arranged to show her a video of a bunch of California skydivers performing their free-fall aerobatics. Compelling as the footage was, it was just as exhilarating to watch Irina with her hand to her heart and her intelligent eyes taking in the outlandish beauty of the skydivers joining in free-fall, making doily-like configurations against a bluebird backdrop.

Irina and I practiced that engaging act in which foreigners relating ideas find their heads almost touching in the tiny space above a two-language pocket dictionary. As we pointed at words for each other we'd come up eye-to-eye and smile at the little epiphany. It is an arduous process nonetheless, and at times it is tempting, especially with a person as completely agreeable as Irina, to just say "Da."

After the video Irina pointed toward the TV and gestured at me, inquiring, I thought, if I liked it. "Da, da, da," I said emphatically because I had been quite taken with the whole show. It was poignant watching this cosmonaut, this world-class skydiver, a woman with more than 5,000 jumps, watch a video of her favorite avocation.

Months later, a painstakingly translated letter arrived from Moscow. It was a formal invitation from Cosmonaut Irina Solovyova and her husband, Lt. Col. Sergei Kiselov, for me to come to the USSR and go skydiving with them as I had requested when I'd watched the video that afternoon in San Francisco. Irina had asked if I'd like to skydive, rather than if I liked the skydiving. This was the first of many misunderstandings that I would experience with Irina and Sergei along the way to my first jump. My knowledge of Russian ran to roughly six words. An ominous footnote to the invitation asked that I come in late winter, when the snow is deepest.

One dreary, windy day in February, Sergei Kiselov met me at Moscow's Sheremetyeva International airport, a dark, cavernous building with what looked like upturned wastebaskets covering the ceiling. We picked up a mutual friend, Ira Kuznetsova, a Russian photojournalist, who had accompanied Irina Solovyova on the Antarctic trek, and we drove an hour north to Star City, home of the cosmonauts and the Soviet Space Program, to rest a bit, get acquainted, and prepare for a weekend of skydiving. As far as I could ascertain, I was the first American ever to be allowed to visit this top-secret Soviet training base.

We spent that first evening in the Star City high rise that houses the cosmonauts. It was the most spacious apartment I've ever seen in Russia. Sergei and Irina's beautiful 20 year old daughter Lena, sat at a sewing machine in the living room serenely humming, making a snow suit of her own design from some white surplus parachute fabric. She spoke English with a slightly French inflection and translated for us while still delighting in sewing her creation. A photo album prompted some brief biographies. Irina Solovyova in her space suit. Irina in an Antarctic blizzard. Irina skydiving. In addition to having been a cosmonaut and polar explorer, Irina Solovyova is a psychologist who helps prepare the new generation of cosmonauts for their space flights.

Their living room is lined with shelves, and in a place of honor, right next to a framed photo of Yuri Gagarin, the first man in space and the best man at their wedding, is a book of photographs of Montana. In 1980, when there was still money for such things, Sergei, as head of the Soviet skydiving team, brought sixty Russians in an Ilyushin cargo plane to Billings, Montana, for a parachuting festival. Sergei, who had recently retired as a colonel in the Soviet Army, coaches the Soviet skydiving team. Choreographer may be a better job description. He designs strategies in which as many as fifty people sprint out the rear door of a huge cargo plane at 17,000 feet. The team members link appendages to form those doily-like configurations as they freefall at 130 MPH, then they separate, pop their chutes, and sedately glide to earth, landing like a flock of geese descending on a cornfield.

Besides teaching every Soviet cosmonaut to parachute, Sergei spent much of his 35 year career in the army as a weightlessness tester. Before any humans experienced weightlessness in space, Sergei had spent countless hours, thirty seconds at a time, flying through giant parabolas in cargo planes, studying this unknown state into which man was inviting himself. Sergei's aerial life seems to have preserved and edified him. He's a rock hard man in his mid-sixties with the step of a 20 year old. His speech utilizes all the drama that the Russian language supports. He seems to end each of his pronouncements to colleagues, family, or friends with his strong chin leading a boyish smile and arched eyebrows inviting agreement. He is the most powerfully affable person I have ever met.

The next day, before leaving Star City, which is home to about 40 cosmonauts and the 5,000 people who train and support them, we went to the only food store inside this walled city that is inhabited by dozens of "Heroes of the Soviet Union," to find provisions for our stay at the Voloslova aerodrome, a Soviet Air Force parachute-training base that doubled as a civilian skydiving center on weekends. One can't assume that there will be food anywhere in Russia these days, and this city of the privileged was our best chance to find some food to go. The state-run store, a blond brick storefront of modest size, had a long queue of stoic folks, many in the coarse wool great coats of the Soviet

Army. After a wait of twenty minutes we got to the front of the line, and Ira remarked how relatively easy life was in this place. None of the shelves for dry goods had a thing on them. We were able to buy six wax paper sandwich bags of boiled fish parts and some almonds. Ira inquired about some bottled milk in a refrigerated display case but was told by a shrugging man that milk is only for those with infants under one year of age. He pointed at a list. We rounded out our supplies with a two-liter jar of stewed tomatoes, a dozen boiled eggs from the reserves at the Kiselov household, and some jerky I had brought along. Irina Solovyova had to work, and said she'd try to join us on Saturday. On a cold, snowy Thursday afternoon in February, Sergei Kiselov, Ira Kuznetsova, and I set out on the two hour ride over the terribly pot-holed Russian roads to go skydiving.

The Soviet aerodrome was barely lit by a few street lamps; most of the light posts were out cold. Our late arrival, however, hadn't gone unnoticed. When the men shuffling out of the stolovaya (mess hall) recognized Sergei's car, there had been a foot-stomping moonlit re-union on the icy footpath in front of the barracks. Sergei, a world champion at the sport with more than 10,500 jumps in his logbook, is something of a legend in this place but he was greeted more as a pal. I didn't understand much more than the spirit of this meeting, but it was another heartwarming example of the dignity and respect with which Russians can treat one another. Comradeship is nurtured. They said the word "comrade" quite a bit and their conversation sounded like buddies getting together, not a hint of brainwashed commies reciting their lines was apparent. I was, of course, completely ignorant of what these men were saying, but I knew I was the subject of some of the discourse, and I was made to feel like a welcome curiosity.

We went into the barracks to a narrow two-bunk room and eight men sat knee to knee under a bare 60-watt light bulb and drank a little vodka. Alexander Parfenov, the most senior of the instructors, opened his tiny refrigerator, revealing half a jar of pickled tomatoes, a slice of bread, some wrapped candy and a sheath knife. True to Russian cus-tom, he insisted we eat his tomatoes and sweets to temper the effects of the vodka he kept tipping into our glasses. A man named Mikhail began rolling cigarettes and handing them out and never stopped and he translated a few phrases for me: "He bolshoi (big) pilot Afghanistan," or "Food, petrol, women, big problem," and, "American number one good jumping. Good man."

Talk turned to the breakup of the central government. The folks at Volosova don't even know who owns the planes they fly and jump from. They are sure that the ground they land on is Russia. But from the ground up, ownership of the aircraft, rolling stock, and even buildings is an open question. The USSR was steadily and swiftly deteriorating and prioritizing who got the scraps was anyone's guess. As long as the Volosova base kept training the paratroopers, they can obtain fuel rations. They get food anyway they can. "They," my comrades for my first jump, are a collection of mostly Afghanistan vets who want to escape the city life anyway they can and they want to fly and jump from airplanes and helicopters every chance they get. They intend to just keep on living like a sort of tribe, like a commune of pilots and skydivers.

About 10PM Mikhail announced he had to catch the bus back to Moscow and the last toast was to "Rooski, Amerikanski, Mir (peace)." The guys on the other cot stood in unison and filed out, then the guys on my side repeated the nearly military exit. It was the only sensible way to move the comrades out of a room not much wider than the door. Everyone trudged across the rutted ice to accompany the departing comrade to the bus stop and the camaraderie, unabated, seemed to be all the warmth anyone could need.

I remembered some things from my own past then, and although I couldn't fathom the nuance of the language, I understood much that night. I spent ten years of my life working with draft horses and heavy equipment logging in the forests of Montana and Oregon. I know the habits and spirit cultivated by people who work with machinery and rigging in life-and-death situations. Our priorities were staying alive and enjoying the work. Money was down the list a ways. That first night in Volosova, in that cold-water barracks, and the icy streets, in the company of men who pursue a monastically simple existence to live as aviators and skydivers, I felt that I was in a safe place with people who take care with each other.

We returned to the barracks and bunked in an unheated room, in our clothes, under worn green wool blankets.

At sunup, Sergei Kiselov's gray-maned silhouette cut a figure of continuous animation in front of the filthy window of our two-cot room. He was fit as a high school swimmer and clearly relishing his role: he was about to instruct me in the rudiments of stepping out of an airplane into the sky 6,000 feet above the earth. Dawn revealed a low ceiling of clouds that released scant, spherical snowdrops that fell straight and fast over the Red Army barracks and sparsely wooded military base that Sergei shrugged over as he caught a handful from the open window. He somehow imparted the fact that the weather might dampen our parachuting prospects. Irrepressibly enjoying the improbable scene between two strangers from differing cultures, Sergei turned and held eye contact, his fresh-shaven chin leading an ever-ready smile, index finger pointed skyward, beyond the tawdry window, and he treated me to his best and only English phrases: "Life is life," he chuckled. He raised his finger higher and bestowed his only other English expression: "Yes oh clock."

Sergei, my new friend, instructor, and jumpmaster has spent a good part of his life plummeting earthward in the rarified air where few birds ever bother to fly. Besides his 35 year career in the Soviet Army spent training aspiring cosmonauts to parachute, he's spent hundreds of hours, in 30 second installments, spread frog-like in unfettered freefalls, plunging more than 10,000 miles through the air, a mile at a time. He has been taking off in airplanes that he didn't land in as a career for three decades. On this frosty morning he instills a sense of discipline by the military dignity he projects as he instructs me in the points I need to know to live through a jump from an airplane. The rather glaring issue that we were adjusting to was our mutual illiteracy, our almost complete ignorance of the others' language. At one point a pilot's Airedale walked into our room and, as Sergei fussed over him, I realized that this dog understood at least a dozen more Russian words than I did.

Undaunted, Sergei began my ground schooling over breakfast. Half an eggshell served as a parachute canopy. He spoke slowly and distinctly as the eggshell repeatedly descended in his steady hand towards a table littered with cracked almond shells, fish parts, and jerky. I assimilated two facts: "Problem" means the same in both languages, and his repetition of the word "Nyet," while making dervish overhead gestures rendered the message that bad things can happen even after the parachute opens. After just a few frustrating minutes of his discourse, we knew we had a definite communication problem. We sat sipping tea; smiling and shrugging at each other knowing my first jump would be a new experience for both of us.

Mercifully, Ira Kuznetsova joined us. Ira had been trying hard to translate, but English is new to her. The hardworking verbs and prosaic nouns of normality don't help much when trying to explain the arcana of parachute hardware, maneuvering in the wind and sky, and techniques for landing safely. Sergei, through Ira's best efforts, was trying to instruct me in what to do between the time I jumped and landed. A taped playback of one of these lessons as articulated by Ira goes: "Red strap work apparat high level. If big not work use. Normal one but two work at one hundred fifty meters." To allay the torturous process Ira was putting herself through I would at times interject, Kahnyeshna, (Sure), or Ya pahneemya, (I understand). To be sure, Sergei's pantomimes, broad gestures, and enactments had instilled in me a sense of the day's possibilities.

Sergei, turning to universal languages, made two pages of drawings and equations in my notebook in an attempt to explain wind velocities, rates of descent, and parachute handling. While he illustrated a body being dragged across the ground, there was a loud knock at the door and a shouted announcement. Sergei thanked the unseen voice, pointed at the ten on my wristwatch, and said, "Yes Oh Clock." He squinted at me and shrugged his shoulders and self-deprecatingly repeated, "Yes oh clock," acknowledging that we sure have a crazy deal going on here. But I definitely wanted to do this by now; as much to satisfy Sergei and this unique connection in my life as to experience something completely new and terrifying that had me antsy and willing. I was told that I was the first American to jump at this paratrooper-training center, probably the first ever in the Soviet Union. That sounded very cool and added to the enticement. Sergei had held forth brightly, playfully, and eagerly about our arrangement to get me under a parachute over the USSR in the winter. Strangely attracted to abnormal doings as I am, I wanted to do this with Sergei. I figured that a million people had done this, that it was a very edgy human activity, and that I was in good hands and it would somehow play out just fine.

I pulled on the outfit he borrowed for me upon our arrival the night before: insulated overalls, tall, lace-up sheepskin-lined black boots favored by Russian skydivers, and a venerable leather aviator's jacket. We walked single-file out into crusty snow and temperatures a few degrees below freezing, following a narrow footpath through the snow behind the barracks. Sergei's silver hair streamed out from under his electric-blue stocking cap, looking as though it hadn't been cut since his retirement a year ago. On the other side of a thicket of young birches and pines a wingless fuselage lay in the snow like a huge broken toy. We quietly climbed in through a four foot wide door on the left side. Sergei had settled for no speech, just gestures, smiles, and seductive winks. He showed me how to place my left foot on the threshold of the fuselage door and had me repeat that move a couple of times. Then he bent slightly, arms folded as though gut shot, and jumped out. He motioned for me to bend and jump on the same spot. When I did, he said, Horosho (good).

We followed another trail through knee-deep snow to a large swing set with half a dozen parachute harnesses hanging from it. Directly under the harnesses the snow was trampled into cratered footprints laid atop one another in the dirty ice. He showed me all the clasps and buckles and I shrugged into a harness. He dangled in the harness next to me showing how to manipulate the four straps (two on each side, one fore and one aft) to make myself twist in the rig. Again I muttered, "Ya pahneemyah," but without feeling too cavalier or even sure what he meant. But, harnesses, whether for alpinists or draft horses, make a sense of their own when the webbing and hardware are hooked up. This harness, with a few adaptations for high winds and the sudden load when the parachute opens, looked respectably over-engineered.

We looked into the parachute-packing room; a well-lit place with a pile of chutes the size of a small haystack at one end awaiting re-packing. Intent teenagers worked on their hands and knees on the clean brown floor straightening and folding while patient instructors hovered over the whole operation. Sergei pointed out an orange parachute and a white one. He tried to tell me something about the two different types of chutes. I again nodded and said, "Da," wondering if he thought I was color blind as he was showing me their distinct colors. Then several unmuffled motors fired up somewhere outside the chute-packing loft. We walked out through a fringe of forest thrumming with the steady racket of 1500 horsepower radial engines warming up. They thundered out there, a quarter mile away, on the vast jump zone that had been hacked out of the thick, tall pine and spruce taiga that had covered this aerodrome site before airplanes were invented. The prop-wash from the four big biplanes blew up a small blizzard out on the airstrip.

At the staging area about 50 paratroopers milled around the stacks of packed chutes laid on canvas ground cloths that were frozen stiff. Some of the soldiers, already strapped into their chutes, sat smoking on the benches that faced the airstrip. A civilian instructor approached, it was Sasha Parfenov, our vodka host from the night before who looked and smelled like he'd kept the party going alone. Sasha held out a parachute and reserve, blinking away smoke from a cigarette poking from the side of his mouth. As he silently buckled me into the harness I shifted my weight, using inertia or subtle motion wherever it helped. He worked intently; putting his eyes and hands on every piece of the rigging at least twice.

When we were ready, Sergei reminded me that Irina Solovyova had advised me to speak into my tape recorder during our ascent. Cosmonauts are required to jump as part of their psychological training and because they land on land rather than at sea, as American spacefarers do. They are generally ejected from their capsules and parachute to Earth from about 17,000 feet. On the ride up for their first jump, Irina had explained, they are told to recite poetry, do simple math, or just record their feelings. Many can't utter a word. My tape recorder was accessible, in a pocket above my knee, and we attached a tiny microphone inside a dust mask I'd wear until it was time to jump out of the plane. Sergei headed towards the idling Antonov, a huge single engine biplane; I followed like an acolyte. A column of about a dozen army paratroopers filed along behind us. Sergei began jogging the last 50 or so meters to the vivid army-green biplane idling out on the snow-packed runway. It sat on skis the size of 20-man toboggans in an upwardly angled yearning-for-flight attitude that makes all tail draggers look like they truly long for the sky.

As I ran behind Sergei to the big ski plane I thought cynically, "Don't keep the machine waiting," and remembered times when loggers I'd known had been injured or killed laboring under the same rationale: working too fast because the idling machinery is waiting. But then I realized Sergei runs playfully. The appropriate pace for approaching an airplane you have decided to jump from is at a run.

The Antonov 2 biplane has been unrivaled since the 1940s for its ability to leap into the air with a pilot and copilot and 14 jumpers and their parachutes. It's a bucolically proportioned workhorse, a kind of an aerodynamic grain truck and the largest single-engine airplane ever built. I described its virtues and homely features into my tape recorder as the plane climbed. Such details as the two steps up into the flight deck, its shiny, bare-aluminum bench seats along both sides, its portholes with faded floral-pattern curtains, and its worthless heating system with little nipples pointing down at each passenger seemed an odd mix of utility, humanity, and the fading hopes of humans whose lives are lived playing up in the sky.

Seated in the huge biplane, facing each other much as we'd been the night before in the barracks, the Red Army paratroopers looked nonchalant. Steady exhalations of frosted breath disappeared between their knees in the center aisle. The trooper next to me, an unshaven man with red-rimmed green eyes, told me in a French/English patois that he had been to Paris once. He seemed to appreciate my attention and he launched a bunch of friendly French my way.

I babbled "interesting" into my tape recorder about a dozen times in that twenty minute ascent. Then I turned the recorder off and stashed the dust mask and microphone in a knee pocket.

Suddenly a klaxon alarm's vibrating bellow penetrated my body and squeezed my adrenal glands, warning that we were approaching the jump zone. At the left rear of the plane a red light glowed on the bulkhead over the shoulder of the burly jumpmaster. He swung the four foot wide door in and secured it, flooding the cabin with light and a swirling, bitterly cold wind. The yellow light over the door started blinking, the klaxon quit and a horn honked intermittently like a leftover alarm from World War Two, and the seven Russian Army paratroopers on the left side rose, snapped carabiners onto a stout cable just below the ceiling, bent slightly, and crabbed towards the open door. Then the steady blare of that damn horn, the steady green light and the head-to-butt line of paratroopers jumped out into the 120

MPH winds and tore off earthward. All of us on the right side rose. Then the six guys ahead of me disappeared out the door. "Pashal... Pashal...Pashal," the jumpmaster yelled as he gave each trooper a last thump on the parachute. Last in line, I placed my left foot on the threshold, grabbed the doorframe, and was making my move when something more terrifying than that doorway started up.

I was jerked back into the plane, spun around and faced with a jumpmaster whose eyes flashed with anger, fear, and surprise. With the open door, the light and wind at my back, and my every cell engorged with adrenaline, my thoughts didn't come in a succession, but flashed in an unconstructed body of fear. Russians. Cold War. Enemies. Outnumbered. They packed my chute. As a child in the 1950s I had been taught to fear what appeared in the sky. Every plane too high to really observe threatened annihilation. Any contrail up there could be a Russian bomber, the nuns at St. Philomena's told us. There was even a civilian corps in Montana, the "Skywatchers" that was trained to watch for Russian bombers that were heading south from the North Pole to wipe us out. Every air raid siren's howling rehearsal served as an implicit reminder that the Rooskies could fry us all anytime they felt compelled. One poster, advertising for Skywatchers, had reminded us that, "The Kremlin has a thousand bombers that can hit your home."

Sergei stepped forward, slowly reached for my hand, and carefully pulled me away from the door. He tapped my wrist altimeter and circled his index finger in an ascending spiral. His eyebrows arched, asking me to understand. His sky blue eyes carefully searched mine. We sat. The pilot, looking down from his perch in the cockpit, gave the thumbs-up and pushed the throttle forward a touch. The Antonov bucked and we banked up into the thin clouds.

I sat cursing inwardly, feeling confused, and embarrassed. As my pulse slowed I regretted my unworthy thoughts and was amazed at the depth of my residual Cold War fears. The jumpmaster reached out the door and gathered in all the static lines that had pulled the paratroopers' chutes open for them. His back to me, shaking his head, he slammed and latched the door, then turned and looked me over. Finally he half-smiled under a rusty walrus mustache and gave me the thumbs-up, a gesture that said, "At least you're willing to jump." It occurred to me that Sergei must have explained that I wasn't supposed to jump with the paratroopers but that this information didn't get through. Perhaps it was in the chute-packing room, when he was showing me the different colored canopies. Sergei was studying me; he tried to act casual, but he remained wide-eyed. After a bit, he winked and nodded soberly, grooming his grey mustache, hiding a grin. I grabbed my mic and recorded my last messages before my first jump. "Lord, if this parachute doesn't work, but reincarnation does, make me a bird, maybe a swallow, an aerial feeder, I want to fly."

When the klaxon brayed again, I knew it was for me. I stood facing Sergei, and in a quick review composed entirely of gestures he reminded me: "Jump. Feet together and strong when you land." The horn pounded through all the other noises. I put my left instep on the edge of the door, felt the slipstream dragging at my toes, saw a strangely tilted landscape far below, felt a padded thump on my parachute, and I jumped.

I was engulfed, unutterably shocked in a grayness in which I was unattached to anything. For a few seconds I was senseless. Then in rapid succession my senses returned. The roar of the Antonov receded. I felt a tug from my crotch through my chest and shoulders, looked up and saw I was at the vortex of a descending spiral of strings suspended from the dirty-white canopy. I laughed out loud when the untwisting shroud lines put an almost comical rag-doll twist on me. I sucked in a deep breath and the air tasted of cinnamon. Then, from above and behind me, I heard Sergei's voice shouting urgently. I pulled the red cord, which I found out later was rigged to disarm the automatic release on my reserve chute.

It was while trying to turn myself by pulling on the big straps at my shoulders that I finally admitted I had learned nothing about parachuting that morning. I managed to turn my body so I could see Sergei under his sports chute canopy. He hollered, "Tom... Tom... Nyet... Nyet," a few more times. My canopy wasn't turning; I had merely, by lifting and twisting myself in the harness, made my body turn. I tried to turn the other direction, grabbing the opposite straps. Then we drifted so far apart I couldn't discern his voice and he quit hollering. I ended up hanging there as limp and useless in flight as a crow's foot. Sergei turned his sky blue chute, a racy-looking rectangular canopy compared to the dirty hemisphere under which I dangled, and he headed back towards the runway.

The aerodrome noises rose faintly from below. A dog barked somewhere down there. From my elevation I could discern the layout of the place. The airfield and jump zone are cut squarely into the vast, forested plain of pines and birches that surrounds Moscow. The barracks, mess hall, parachute-packing rooms and other buildings are scattered throughout the forest at the southern edge of the airfield.

As I floated down to this backwoods Russian aerodrome I felt elated, I was in the sky with only fabric, cords, straps and some buckles keeping me up there and I knew this essentially untutored jump was not the least impulsive, it was the realization of a lifelong desire for that bird's eye look at the earth, but, more than that, I had not let Sergei down. I was to learn much later that I had passed a test designed to help my new Russian friends gauge how some mutual trust might build. The cosmonauts and Afghan veterans were testing and watching me in order to determine whether or not they would, or could, entice me to return to their world and build friendships.

Then the forested edges of the airfield and jump zone widened beyond comprehension and I stared down at the patch of hard-packed snow coming at me fast. When I was at the height of a five-story building I locked my legs together, bent and tensed them. I had to concentrate to maintain the isometric tension in my knees, as the snowfield seemed to rush up at me way too fast. It's obvious from the swiftness of the descent that the landing will be hard, but while still suspended you are tensing all those muscle groups against nothing. No fall I have ever taken could have prepared me for the landing.

When I landed, my velocity wasn't increasing. It's not as I'd imagined, like jumping from a garage or some other stationary height. This was like stepping backward off the top tier of a loaded hay truck. My ignorance of parachuting again left me to my own devices. I didn't collapse my parachute when I landed. The breeze-filled canopy dragged me across the snow for about 100 feet until I pulled in a few arm's-lengths of shroud lines closest to the ground. I clamped my teeth on the lines while I reached ahead to grab some more. The idea was to collapse the canopy by depriving it of its volume as I pulled it out from under itself. The snow-coated shroud lines between my teeth gave me a sense of cold accomplishment as if the more tooth and claw required, the better.

Finally the canopy collapsed and I got to my feet. I shed my harness and emptied the snow that had been plowed up inside my jacket. I realized why "come when the snow is deep," was so prominent in the initial invitation. I rolled up my parachute as Sergei had shown me in a drawing that morning. He walked up with his own gear already stowed and slung over his shoulder and helped me stuff my chute into the bag that had been lashed under my reserve chute. We were careful not to let too much snow get in the bag with the parachute. "Tom," he said standing back a bit and smiling a benediction, "Mala Dyetz...Mala Dyetz" (Fine fellow...fine fellow). We dropped our gloves in the snow, laughed, shook hands, and jerked each other into a backslapping bear hug under the overcast sky.

When we turned to walk back to the staging area, Sergei had the good taste not to acknowledge the strange slash of a track I left when I was dragged through the snow. In the foot of crusted snow with the awkward burden of the big canopies and harness, his step was light. He ignored the dozens of parachutists descending towards us. The quarter-mile walk back to the staging area, after our 9,000 foot fall, gave me a good inventory of my moving parts. I truly had survived and wanted only to jump again.

Back at the staging area, a bunch of people congratulated me and I was given the medal Soviet Army paratroopers receive that commemorates their first jump. Sergei introduced me to Irina Tivelkova, wife of the chief of the aerodrome. Irina speaks the English peculiar to parachuting very well. She quickly explained that I wasn't supposed to jump with the paratroopers because I was using a different canopy, one that drops faster, and that I could have fallen on one of them and collapsed his chute. She also explained the use of the red straps for turning the canopy, and that the big straps were only for last second adjustments for landing safely. She added sweetly, "People are watching you. We are fond of our first American parachutist."

I was helped into another parachute and, at the front of another column of paratroopers, I jogged over the snow and ice to an idling Antonov. Again I spoke into my recorder on the way up. Sergei had taped the microphone under a proper face mask and, hands-free, I even blathered some impressions as I descended. As I rolled and bundled my parachute, and ambled back to the staging area the cloud cover lowered over the Russian steppes, the surface winds increased, and the window for safe jumping closed at about noon. Sergei, Ira Kuznetsova, and I went back to the barracks for tea and lunch.

While we waited for some water to boil, Sergei asked, through Ira, if we could listen to the "reportage" in my recorder. Ira said she'd try to translate if I could make the playback pause. My voice came across the background clamor of engine noises, klaxon, and wind pretty clearly from inside the face mask with the microphone. We laughed at all the times I said "interesting." My descriptions of the aerodrome, the people, the hardware, aircraft, and weather, however, sounded oddly terse, too detached from all the exhilaration.

Sergei seemed agitated. He fingered his forehead with both hands and then placed his right hand over his heart. He said he was curious about my emotional experience as I had jumped out of an airplane into the Soviet Union. I lamely explained that my job as a journalist doesn't usually include my personal feelings. He said, "Your emotions today might be important for you to remember." He glanced down at an egg he was holding, then fixed me with a placid smile. "Tom, we are learning to trust," he said, watching me carefully. "We jump to understand trust."

This wiry birdman of a retired Soviet Army Colonel sat peeling hardboiled eggs and allowed me my dignity as I leaned over, head in my hands. In those few words he truly dispelled the Cold War. A lifetime of Russophobia learned from all the fervent nuns, cunning politicians, and made constant in the media and by the Skywatchers, washed out of me in a tearful purge. I had come here with Sergei unable to communicate at all verbally. I trusted him unconditionally and put my life in his hands. He had just lightened it and shined it and handed it back.

I tried to write down my feelings. I didn't feel macho or adventurous. You can't muscle your way through a one-mile fall. Jumping was a cogent choice insofar as I had managed a series of incremental acts that a person I trusted wanted me to accept. Acceptance accumulates.

I wrote that all I learned on a physical level that day was the terrible willingness of a fledgling upon that first step from the nest. I thought at the time, and still do after hundreds of subsequent jumps in Russia, that skydiving is, as they say, fearfully absurd, a violation of instinctive precepts of survival. But it is controllable. It's something to get to know. As practiced and taught by Sergei Kiselov, skydiving is life giving, an act suffused with heart.

Free-falling with Frightful Franklin

(previously published in Smithsonian Air & Space)

Author Note: In 2004 I pitched this feature article about the fastest animal on Earth to Smithsonian Air & Space magazine. Linda Shiner, the Senior editor, agreed that they'd like to see it, after I'd contributed about 20 previous articles. My fondness for Ken and Suzanne Franklin and their peregrine falcon, "Frightful," kind of leaked out all over my writing. I still keep in touch with them.

She perches on a bald tire in Ken and Suzanne Franklin's country kitchen. "Frightful," a peregrine falcon, is just being herself, loudly "cacking" and occasionally opening her wings to their 44-inch span. She flaps those wings and stretches a little and preens herself with her hooked beak. Frightful catches other birds in midair for a living, more precisely, she slams into them at more than 200 M.P.H. and chases their falling bodies to the ground and dines on them. She ignores a piece of barbecued chicken that is within reach. She watches everything that moves. Frightful is a world-class athlete, the fastest directly recorded animal that has ever lived. When "stooping," diving after their prey from as high as 14,000 feet, peregrine falcons attain higher velocities than any other animal on earth. Until recently speculation on their velocity varied wildly; from 70 to 300 MPH. Given that peregrines are the most-studied birds on earth—they live on every continent but Antarctica—such a void in our knowledge attests to how difficult it is to closely observe falcons in flight. No one had ever measured and recorded exactly how fast the birds could fly until Ken Franklin started stooping with Frightful, or more to the point, Frightful took to sky-diving with Ken.

"Studying falcons from the ground is like studying sharks from a boat," Ken says. Certain risks lurk when humans enter a predator's element for the purpose of observation. But Ken, with support from Suzanne, Roy Franklin, his father, several other falconers, two film making crews, and Norman Kent, the world-renowned skydiving videographer, has undertaken a study of high-speed falcon stooping literally, at arm's length. For the sake of understanding how a two-pound bird can fly at speeds in excess of 240 MPH, Ken has executed as many as six skydives a day with Frightful.

"Birds are the blueprint for aeronautical engineering," says Ken, a 46 year old master falconer from Friday Harbor, Washington. A commercial pilot who first took the controls of an airplane at age nine, Ken wants to apply aspects of what he has measured and discovered skydiving with falcons to mechanized flight. "What remains to be learned? Can human flight benefit from these observations?" he asks.

Reflecting in 1941, on how he had benefited from observing birds in flight, Orville Wright wrote, "Learning the secret of flight from a bird was a good deal like learning the secret of magic from [watching] a magician." Not content to learn about falcons in flight from the mezzanine, so to speak, Ken Franklin, at considerable risk and expense, has made more than 200 skydives with peregrine falcons.

John Szabo, a theoretical mathematician for NASA, and a master falconer who works closely with the Franklins, says, "What Ken is observing while freefalling with peregrines from 17,000 feet is unique in the history of humans studying flight." Since Ken's freefall studies commenced in 1998, he has verified that peregrine falcons are the fastest creatures on Earth. Ken has witnessed and measured Frightful in a vertical dive at 242 MPH.

To record precise, repeatable, indisputable data on the velocity that Frightful attains, Ken and a group of mathematicians and engineers stripped down a skydiver's Protek recording altimeter, an instrument usually worn like a wristwatch, to a 13-gram computer chip that could be fastened to the underside of Frightful's tail feathers without interfering with her flight. In dozens of skydives in 1999, while shooting the National Geographic film, "Terminal Velocity," Franklin and his team measured stooping speeds and calibrated and verified recordings of Frightful's stoops against the Protek altimeters worn by Ken and videographer Norman Kent. A fourth recording altimeter was packed into a lure that could fall faster than the skydivers that Frightful pursued when Ken, freefalling, dropped it just before opening his parachute at 5,000 feet above the Strait of Juan de Fuca, where the Pacific Ocean mixes with the waters of Puget Sound. All four altimeters equated after each of dozens of jumps.

On the ground, Ken Franklin looks like Sam Sheppard on a bad hair day, as though all those skydives have permanently startled his shock of brown hair. He roams his 14 acre farm like a raptor, his shoulders still and his head thrust forward, as though hunting up a meal. In the sky, Ken is as facile and experienced as any human can be. He has logged more than 17,000 hours in the cockpits of just about every type of aircraft including 747s and MD11s for the Flying Tigers and FedEx. At 21, he was the youngest pilot ever hired by a commercial airline. Arrayed around his farmhouse and sheds are two Cessnas, a Robinson R22 helicopter, two ultra lights, and a few parachutes that he has used to log more than 1900 skydives, including a couple hundred freefalls with falcons. His experience training and flying with falcons predates such magnificent efforts as the movie Winged Migration, and he has garnered enough attention to merit the National Geographic film, as well as an IMAX movie produced by Roy Disney. But the disciplines of aeronautical engineering and airflow dynamics have largely ignored his findings, which he has offered freely to share with the world of commercial aviation.

The late Dr. Jim Crowder, Airflow Fellow at Boeing, a leading authority on the airflow dynamics of wings and control surfaces, lamented the lack of interest elicited by the aviation industry for closer studies of the aerodynamic properties of bird flight, and, particularly, the peregrines. In June, 2000, referencing Franklin's studies in freefall with peregrines, Crowder wrote: "Regarding applicability to commercial aviation, that is a tough question. The easy answer, if talking about Boeing-type aviation, is 'no.' Our (Boeing) position is that aviation is a mature business and that any discoveries waiting to be identified are probably not worth looking for, much less implementing. Someone would have found them by now." Dr. Crowder's lament was his addendum to this corporate indifference to Franklin's years of study with peregrines in freefall. "Personally, I am convinced that birds do all kinds of things that are unknown and potentially worth finding out about," Crowder wrote. "I have spent my entire career inventing and innovating equipment and testing methods. All too frequently I am asked, 'What good is it?' My usual answer is 'Nothing at all unless you think about it.'"

That birds in flight are thought provoking to aviators is obvious. Ken Franklin has been observing, training, and thinking about falcons most of his life. At age twelve he captured and began training a red-tailed hawk. He'd take the hawk to his father's 66-acre airport adjacent to Friday Harbor where it caught rabbits and smaller rodents. Falconry became a lifelong avocation. Coupled with his career in commercial aviation, it was inevitable that he began to wonder how his observations of bird flight, accumulated over decades, might offer improvements in mechanical flight. Then he acquired Frightful and knew he had the bird he'd dreamed about.

Frightful "Franklin" is an "imprinted" peregrine falcon. Within two days of hatching she was swept in to the center of Franklin family, to the extent that she regards Ken and Suzanne's king-sized bed her nest. She often spends hours perched on a ledge above the kitchen counter. She can be raucous, "cacking" loudly and flapping her wings when she is stimulated or displeased, such as when a bearded reporter for Air & Space shows up at her elbow, so to speak. "Most imprinted falcons are namby pamby," Ken says when he pauses from vocalizing with Frightful. "Frightful got her name because she is the closest thing to a wild falcon that I've ever trained." She also regards Ken as her mate-for-life. She would allow him, and only him, to the exclusion of male falcons, to inseminate her. "Training techniques are all about feeding and breeding," Ken says. Her instincts to fly with her mate, especially when ostensibly in pursuit of food, made her partner up with Ken on training jumps with alacrity. There is a sense of precision and trust when Ken or Suzanne handles Frightful, a sense that is wholly different when, say, a reporter warily offers his gloved fist as a perch for the two-pound bird. "Tilt your wrist a few degrees, until you feel her settle," Suzanne instructs. "Feel her."

A "haggard," or mature falcon, Frightful has stiff, unyielding feathers. She is roughly the size and shape of a loaf of French bread. With her wings tucked away and her feathers lying flat against her she feels as firm as a football. Every feather on her body has a saw toothed, jagged edge that tapers into nothingness. She can flex her feathers individually or in groups, an ability that allows her to make minute corrections at high velocity. Frightful flies effectively in any attitude. Occasionally she flips over, out of a 150 MPH vertical stoop, and awaits her prey in midair as it ineluctably falls into her talons, unable to pull out of its own dive with such agility.

When Ken and Frightful do vertical dives together they are falling 1000 feet every six seconds; flying about 140 MPH. That is terminal velocity—when the weight of a falling object equals the air pressure against it—for a human in a skintight jumpsuit with a parachute strapped on.

In the first few dozen freefalls that Frightful did with Ken, she learned to stoop at exactly his terminal velocity. "She was using her landing gear to regulate her speed to match mine," Ken recalls. Then, while freefalling, Ken began releasing lures that could fall in the 195 MPH range. Frightful began tucking into increasingly aerodynamic shapes and pursuing and catching the lures. Ultimately she began overtaking lures capable of falling more than 240 MPH. At that speed she is flying the length of a football field, including end zones, faster than you can say, "football field." Franklin describes her configuration when going into "hyper drive" as asymmetric; she deforms her shoulders as a human would who is trying to squeeze through a very small opening. "She's slipping through molecules," Franklin says, "The asymmetry seems to be part of that." He holds no hope that airplanes will imitate the malleability and asymmetry of which falcons are capable. But his years of study and observation of falcons all over the world lead him to suggest that replicating certain aspects of peregrine conformation could improve aircraft efficiency.

Franklin's peregrine peregrinations have taken him to South and Central America, Asia, Australia, Europe, the Middle East and several times to Alaska where he had studied nesting falcons. He witnessed the inertial navigational abilities of a gyrfalcon disappearing from a cliff side eyrie into an Aleutian fog that obscured objects ten feet away, only to return unerringly to its nest half an hour later with sushi for the family. Avian homing ability, residing in instinct, may be beyond human understanding. "What exactly goes on in a bird brain may be undecipherable to humans," Ken says.

Suzanne Franklin, who retains the physique of a competitive swimmer, is also a master falconer and ornithologist. She helped Ken devise the incremental training regime that led to numerous skydives with birds eager to participate. To train Frightful as a skydiving partner Ken started flying low and slow in an ultra-light over the grass landing strip on his 14-acre farm a couple miles west of Friday Harbor. Suzanne would hold the hooded bird until Ken made a pass and then she'd pull off the hood and release her. Frightful consistently and unhesitatingly chased the ultra-light in pursuit of the lure Ken held that had some fresh quail meat on it, and perhaps, to fly with the human she regards as her mate. It was a natural progression for Ken to take her up in his Cessna 172, with his father Roy at the controls, to do some freefalling with the falcon in order to closely observe the flight characteristics of a stooping falcon. It is a daunting, improbably wonderful sight to witness Ken gently slipping the hood off Frightful's head and releasing her into the Cessna slipstream at 17,000 feet, and to see her stabilize immediately in level flight and match the speed of the airplane. She flies just off the wingtip, watching Ken inside the plane as he prepares to dive out the door.

Some researchers, all ground-bound observers of falcons, have called Ken's studies artificial, declaring that giving a peregrine a ride so that she is stooping from 17,000 feet is eliciting unnatural behavior. He responds that it is for the benefit of a minute's worth of observation during freefall that he goes so high. "Falcons can accelerate from 100 MPH to 200+ MPH in eight seconds in pursuit of prey," Franklin says. "They don't need that vertical space to accelerate. But they often ride thermals up to cloud base, getting a free ride up the column of air, checking out everything in the airspace for a meal. They soar at altitude, practically invisible, waiting for prey, and then they stoop. To say that stooping from 14,000 plus feet is not normal for a falcon is like observing a Ferrari on a crowded freeway doing 55 MPH and assuming that's all they can do."

John Szabo has calculated that when Frightful, weighing 2.2 pounds, pulls out of high-speed stoops clutching the nearly two-pound lure, she undergoes 27 g's: she and her prize momentarily weigh slightly more than one hundred pounds. Szabo admits that studying a falcon's ability go asymmetric to attain terminal velocity or measuring their ability to endure enormous g forces are probably of no use to commercial aviation. Exploring the mystery of inertial navigation that birds are capable of may be beyond our ken, as we say. But Ken Franklin and John Szabo's research, mathematical modeling, measurements, and observations of falcons in vertical dives lead them to believe that mitigating turbulence, which compromises the efficiency of any type of flight, is possible by applying an aspect of falcon conformation; the jagged edge of their feathers, to airplane skin.

Szabo, whose work for NASA includes computational fluid mechanics that apply to micro surface management, talks about how nature is full of hints at how to move through air and water more efficiently, that is, creating less turbulence, and how humans seem slow to understand how things work. "Look at dolphin and shark skin, for instance," Szabo says. "It wasn't until the 2000 Olympics that the obvious advantage of minuscule dimples in swimsuits could radically improve efficiency over smooth suits by more effectively diffusing turbulence. Altering the design of swimsuits took a cross-disciplinary approach."

The jagged edges at the end of falcon feathers diffuse turbulence by releasing the flow of air less abruptly than a squared-off edge. "Look at the wake turbulence behind a canoe compared to a row boat with a square transom," Szabo says.

Creating a stamped or incised surface that replicates the microscopic unevenness or jaggedness of falcon feather tips, could in John Szabo and Ken Franklin's estimation, improve the efficiency of aircraft significantly. "Look at how vortex generators have revolutionized aviation," Ken says. "There's still room for improvement in drag reduction." Giving a smooth wing surface a bumpy texture resulting in a more slippery passage through the air is counter intuitive until a cross-disciplinary approach is taken. Szabo and the Franklins are not the only researchers suggesting as much.

Scientists at 3M have studied drag reduction and have identified significant potential savings. 3M has developed an adhesive film with a micro structured texture that, when applied to aircraft, will reduce drag, resulting in greater fuel efficiency. Even a 1 percent reduction in fuel use for a wide-body aircraft, as the company points out on its website, equates to about $100,000 in annual fuel savings per aircraft.

Ken and Suzanne Franklin would love to see their observations and studies contribute to aircraft efficiency. They are on the cusp of recognition by serious scientists. On September 19, 2004, Ken will address a meeting for Boeing engineers and the British Royal Society of Aeronautical Engineers, at the Boeing Museum in Seattle.

In an article published in the North American Falconer's Association a few years ago, Ken wrote, "There's merit in dreams and idle speculations. Dreams are the processes by which the imagination eventually inspires the development and procurement of real science."

90 P. S. I.

(previously published in Sports Illustrated, September 8, 1985.)

Author Note: This is the essay Sports Illustrated fact-checked and published, which led to my decision to write for a living.

I own a Denver Broncos trophy buckle and bragging rights to a record that has stood since 1983 and, at the time of this writing, remains an N.F.L. record. The inscription on the silver buckle reads, "90 P.S.I." and is sterling evidence of what is probably the most arcane record hanging around the periphery of the game: catching a football plummeting at about 140 miles per hour. It's time the story is told.

As a logger, or more specifically, a "timber faller," I used to spend most of the year with my hands curled around a 36 pound chainsaw with a 32 inch bar on it. I'd been packing such saws on those steep, snow blanketed Montana Rockies through three months of early winter when I decided to hang up the hardhat and head to Denver with my wife and kids for a Christmas holiday. Most of my eight brothers and sisters would be there, including my brother Bill who worked as the equipment manager for the Broncos in those days. As we drove south through Wyoming, we listened to the 1983 A.F.C. Wildcard game at Seattle. It dampened that Christmas Eve ride to hear Denver going down 31-7.

The next afternoon, when we got to Grandma's, Bill was already back from Seattle, sitting in the living room, looking ambivalent about the sudden end to the season. But he was his same old taciturn self: shrugging off defeat and just enjoying all the wee cousins, watching them play with their new toys and games.

Christmas night after supper, the conversation around the table got Bill cornered, with the rest of us trying to coax bits of Bronco's locker room gossip. It's hard to think of his dealings with those athletes as humdrum, but he rarely had much to say about what his days were like. However, that night he began describing a "football cannon" that the Broncos were using for punt and kick-off return practice.

The machine used compressed air to shoot footballs. Ten pounds per square inch (p.s.i.) would launch the ball 60-70 yards in a fair imitation of a good kick. But boys will be boys, and somebody got the idea to let the compressor run up to the 90 p.s.i. redline and point the barrel straight up to see what would happen. Bill said the ball nearly disappeared before it came back down. Then somebody decided to try to catch the ball when it came screaming back to earth. "Funniest thing I've ever seen at work," he said. Guys that made millions of dollars catching footballs were unable to handle this leather meteorite. "It'd hit them in the hands and just blow their arms apart," Bill laughed. When Rich Karlis, the plucky barefoot kicker tried to catch one, it hit him on the helmet, knocked him down, bounced and landed on the roof of a warehouse across the street. Bill said that the ball had to be doing at least 300 miles an hour.

"Baloney, Bill," I said. I told him that every falling object has a terminal velocity, when the weight of the falling object equals the air pressure against it, and that by quick mental calculation I reckoned the velocity for a football was less than 160 miles per hour. Then, before I had to start backing up my theory with more dubious math, I said, "I could catch it."

The derision in his chortle was as lumpy as the turkey gravy.

"I could catch it, Bill," I repeated, and threw in some amateur psychology, again, hoping to move away from improvising math. "Those big prima donnas are psyching themselves out just because they've never seen a football coming at them that fast. Even with Elway throwing it at them," I said, "When's that kid going to learn a little touch?" I added, imploringly. "Anyway, I have the advantage of not knowing the difference. I could do it if I got five chances."

"Tom, I'd bet you any amount of money. It can't be done. You can't do it. Fifty bucks, no, five hundred bucks ..." He was a little steamed by my naivete and, perhaps, at the suggestion that his guys weren't quite invincible.

"I won't take your money," I replied, "but I'd sure like to have a go. Five tries?"

"You're on. Come on out tomorrow morning at ten."

Bill has a way of looking at you that he's cultivated in locker rooms full of enormous men who must be browbeaten once in a while. I tried not to wither like a chastised linebacker and wondered if maybe the terminal velocity of a football might well be three hundred miles per hour.

The next day the temperature hung at about zero, and there were a few inches of new snow. Nice weather to work in if you're logging, and this was level ground.

Bill set the cannon up on the edge of the practice field nearest the clubhouse. He got the compressor going at the edge of the pure, flat snow-blanketed expanse. There were a few players in parkas, guys cleaning out lockers, who were walking between the parking lot and the locker room. A few guys said they were waiting for some latecomers to go duck hunting. They hung around watching Bill set the football cannon up. "Let's see where they tend to come down," he suggested.

When he shot the first ball up and I watched it disappear into the Denver smog, it set me back some. It's whistling descent hit the snow and blew out a three foot diameter bare spot, as though a cherry bomb had been set off, and bounced thirty yards back towards us. It had burst a seam, leaving what resembled a Labrador scrotum herniating through the split in a seam.

But it was the altitude the ball had reached that left me bemused. I've cut down thousands of trees after walking around them, looking up to see which way they lean. Then they hit the ground, and after I'm done limbing them up and measuring and bucking the saw logs, I know within a few feet how tall they were. As a sideline, I climb 300 foot tall radio towers to replace the burnt-out beacons on top. I can judge heights that have some correlation to human activity. But that ball disappearing into the dirty air and ripping back down to the ground was unlike anything I could relate to. It was like seeing something dropped from an airplane and I guessed it fell 700-800 feet.

Bill shot a couple more footballs up so I could get into the general area where they were rocketing down. I could see them shifting through different wind strata as they returned to earth.

Then one came near enough for me to try to catch it and it hurt my left thumb. But I could see how a few more tries would teach me enough to get the job done. It was like the first time I rode a bull at the jackpot rodeo at Helmville, Montana. Crazy, but exciting and fun and I wanted to keep trying until I got it right.

The second ball that I tried to catch tore the fingernail off my left index finger and bent the whole works up. Bill saw the blood and shut off the compressor, which hissed as it bled off its holding tank.

"This is crazy. We're done," he said.

"It looks worse than it is. Deal's a deal, Bill. I get three more tries."

I was pretty jacked up—there was an audience of guys who'd tried and failed to do this and the implicit challenge was all I could think about. Also, I have read some books about centered skiing and inner golf and tennis, and I believe in that stuff.

While the compressor pumped itself back up, so did I. What you do is imagine a root growing right down through yourself into the ground and then you pull energy into wherever you want it and you start feeling much stronger. I locked my hands together and tucked my elbows against my ribs and concentrated on all the strength that I'd accumulated in those years of lugging chainsaws around on the steeps. When that next ball came down I was moving my feet better, to keep under it as it tumbled down out of the smog and became more vivid and grew in size. It lodged in the cradle that my arms and chest formed. It felt like an 80-pound bale dropped from the hay loft when it hit me and blasted the air out of me, but I held onto it. It knocked me over backwards and my hat landed several feet away. No one doubted that it was a clean catch. The lumpen crowd of jocks in down coats hooted, their applause muted by gloved hands. In this life I spend mostly working around trees I have never elicited applause. I felt very happy.

Every once in a while you have to be your own hero: whether it's being the best snow shoveler on your block, or knowing you're raising kids as polite as can be, or just having a sense of yourself as still being playful and a little crazy. I explained that to Bill and thanked him for setting the deal up. I reached in my pocket for my gloves and found that I couldn't grasp them with my left hand.

Steve Antonopulous, the prematurely bald, wizard trainer for the Broncos, looked at my hand and murmured something and had me stick my hand in ice water for 15 minutes. "Cryotherapy", he called it. There's a loaded word for you. He manipulated my fingers slightly and said I better get to a doctor. Besides tearing my fingernail off, he told me, he was pretty sure that I had broken bones in my left thumb and index finger.

Bill was sorry and a little angry that what had started out to be fun had turned painful. But we talked about all the times we'd seen athletes play with injuries, only to realize they were hurt much later. The human body can take a lot while the mind is engaged energetically.

About a month later, Bill was at a meeting in Cleveland for all the equipment managers in the NFL. It was a huge trade show where he goes to buy everything the team needs for the next season. The average NFL team, for instance, consumes a semi-trailer load of adhesive tape every year. At the closing banquet each equipment manager was called upon to give an impromptu address; sing a song, tell a joke, whatever. Bill asked the assembled team representatives how many had the football cannon. Every team has one. He asked if they'd ever pointed it straight up, at 90 p.s.i.. They all had. He asked if anyone had ever caught the ball. No one had, nor did anyone offer an opinion that it was possible. And, in fact, every team's coaches had banned such idiocy. So Bill told them that his brother, this logger from Montana, had made the catch. He realized, then, that my catch, in its own obscure fashion, was an NFL record.

"Whenever a Bronco establishes a new NFL record they receive a trophy buckle," he wrote on the back of his business card that he'd stuck in the heavy little box the buckle came in. That was about the time I got my cast off. I interpreted this terrific gift, and the trenchant message, as brotherly love, which sweetened the whole thing. I lost a couple months work while that cast was on. That silver buckle cost me about 4,000 dollars in lost wages. But I sure like to tell this story.

Bare Bones Barnstorming

(previously published in Smithsonian Air & Space)

Author note: An unassigned piece that my boss, Linda Shiner, chose to publish in 1996.

My old pal Denny Almendinger sat next to me at the Avon Ladies' softball game the other day telling me how he darn near killed himself and Peggy, flying his two-seater Skye Ryder. "Power lines," he said sheepishly, "you can't forget about them goddang power lines."

The week before, Pat Hansen, a reporter for the Silver State Post in Deer Lodge, had wanted to photograph him flying this contraption. He flew low, so Pat could get some photographs above Spotted Dog road of Denny and his wife, Peggy, in the back seat. He forgot about the power lines that run up to Hank Kertulla's ranch. "The back wheels kind of bumped over the wires," he explained. "Peggy didn't say nothing. She thought I knew what I was doing."

Several times over the last couple of months I've seen Denny flying this powered parachute, this aero chute. It's a form of flight too new to have a generic name. The Skye Ryder is a three-wheeled go-cart-sized outfit with a motor and pusher propeller mounted behind the pilot's head like one of those swamp-skimming air boats. In flight the tubular aluminum framework that supports the pilot, motor, and propeller hangs under a fabric wing big enough to cover a trailer house. When I had gone for the second time to look at it down at Denny's shop, I loaned him my skydiver's wrist altimeter because he was flying the thing with nothing but a tachometer that told him how fast the two-stroke engine was revolving, moot information it seemed to me, since the motor sits right behind his head.

Denny and I kept up the flying-talk, appreciating the flat calm morning. A few low cumulus clouds idled over the Garnet Range foothills that abut Avon's softball field. Cumulus clouds are those blossoms of condensing water vapor that form atop columns of rising thermal air. In the morning they live and die quickly; a wisp of white will grow like slow popcorn and billow, cool, and dissipate in 20 minutes, before they arise and coalesce into thunder bumpers. They are the tell-tales of rising air that various predatory birds use to ascend without flapping a wing.

A freight train rumbled by the right field fence; its clattering passage dominated the narrow valley's acoustics. The gals played on without chatter.

The Avon Ladies don't have a sponsor or uniforms, but they all try to wear green tops. Many of them wear shorts and slide purposefully into the bases, abrading their legs and thighs without regard. They have two bats that they use for games. They don't sport many spiked shoes and designer sunglasses, but they were having their way with the tonier Seeley Lake bunch, in their uniform shirts and matching baseball pants. The most compelling part of the game was the lousy umpiring by Brian Persons, who didn't know about the infield fly rule, and who seemed to believe that merely acting officious would carry the day.

Finally, Denny said, "You're a skydiver Harp. You wanna fly it?"

I didn't answer him. I thought about telling him that I had to go home right now and mow the lawn, or start the barbecue, or set fence posts. I didn't jump into this deal brashly. But the sky looked enticing, like a good day for skydiving. Wondering what it would be like to take off under a parachute canopy and ascend and fly around up there was titillating. I got the butterflies.

Denny didn't press me. We watched another inning. We kept looking up, assessing the nascent cumulus puffs up there that would coalesce into thunder cells by late afternoon.

"Nice sky," Denny said, "Should stay good for a couple hours." My heartbeat steepened.

"Yeah. Okay," I blurted. There it was. There was no sense in putting this off. I'd known since that golden evening when I watched Denny fly east from town, a couple hundred feet above the Little Blackfoot River, and turn and cover the two miles up to my place above the valley in a few minutes; I wanted to try to fly this thing.

Play had stopped. The Avon Ladies were heatedly trying to educate the ump on when to call a hit a foul. Neither Denny nor I wanted to be there when these disgruntled gals with their two aluminum bats looked around for a replacement ump.

Finally: "You'd really let me take her up, Denny?"

"Sure," he said as easily as though he were loaning me a lug wrench. "C'mon, I'll show you how to take off."

We sidled away from the ball game and walked through Henry Price's backyard and across Harpole road to Denny's big brown shop where he works on his silver Peterbilt log truck, his Timberjack log skidder, a Caterpillar road grader, and the various dump trucks, pickups, and chainsaws he uses in his logging business. I used to see a lot more of Denny when I was still logging back in the 70's and early 80's, and I wanted to hang around with him and his alarming new flying machine. We've both operated everything from cranes to Ditch Witches and guys like us want to climb the learning curve that machinery offers.

Denny is a steadfast logger, he makes goods money. Nosed up to his doublewide mobile home is a white Mitsubishi 3000 GT, the most exotic car ever in our little town. But that sports car couldn't sate a middle-aged logger's adrenaline addiction, and sitting in a corner of his cavernous shop are two of these Skye Ryders; a bright green single-seater, and the white tandem for him and Peggy. They were as eye-catching as a car wreck and they looked about as substantial as a K-mart chaise lounge. Three spiffy little chrome wheels with wheelbarrow-sized tires support a triangular framework of inch-and-a-quarter tubing. Denny broke the factory axles in some bad landings, but he has fabricated some beefed-up ones, and the welds seem to be holding, he told me. The orange plastic school lunchroom seat had a maroon Chevrolet seat belt buckled over it. A triangular frame rising behind the seat holds the two-stroke motor. A stuff sack the size of a hay bale hanging from the propeller cage contained the fabric wing under which I would soon be suspended in the sky. The welded tubular framework looked capable in a birdlike way. It looked bare bones light. The thing looked like something a child would draw, believing it would fly. Denny grabbed the chest-high tubular framework that encircles the three-foot diameter propeller. He rocked the little bird lovingly and said, "Pretty good deal, huh?"

I often write about aviators and find that as a group they are dignified, methodical, and articulate people who acknowledge how essential trust is to flight. Denny has a renegade dignity about him and possesses the methodical patience required to repair the complex machinery he owns. He is not, however, as articulate as, say, an Air Force Academy graduate. But it seemed as though he trusted me to fly his little machine.

He explained flying this device without device: "Just sit down on it," he said. I sat in the slippery, hard plastic bucket seat as he engulfed the throttle handle in his grease-seamed paw. "Pretty simple," he said, "you want to go up, push the throttle forward. Pull back and you'll come down. Go easy on it." He had me stretch my legs out to a pair of three-foot-long pipes that were hinged out from the footrests above the front wheel. Attached to their ends were red toggle-lines like those with which skydivers control parachutes. "Push with your foot on the side you want to turn to," he said. "What the hell, Harp, you'll know what to do." He pointed at the tubular stick with a bicycle handgrip between my knees that turns the nose wheel. "Then there's taxiing," he said, like he was using a new word, "Ya kinda bend the stick the way you want to go. It'll pretty much go straight by itself."

He mixed some gas and oil together in a two-gallon gas can and shook it and said, "Enough fuel for a good hour. But don't get caught up there if the wind picks up."

He pulled the starter rope that dangled above the seat. The engine coughed and stuttered up to a racket somewhere between a big chainsaw and a small snowmobile. The whole frame shook and surged, and I anchored my feet in the gravel. He foot-chocked a back wheel and as it warmed up he messed with the idle screw on the tiny carburetor, his round, sunburned face unperturbed, hovering a couple inches from the whirring propeller, as he altered the howl of the two-stroke engine with delicate twists of a screwdriver he'd inserted into the guts of the carburetor. "That's a float carburetor," He hollered, "Don't go flying upside down. Ha Ha." Then he killed the shoebox-sized two-stroke motor, which emitted two devilish belches of gray vapors that rose like smoke signals on a windless morning.

Denny took my seat and without looking he reached up behind his head and restarted the engine in one pull and hollered at me to run across the highway and open the gate to Earl Knight's hay meadow that runs along everyone's backyards on the north side of town. Slouched in the plastic seat, he goosed the wee engine, and turned down Harpole road and blew gaudy candy wrappers the school kids had dropped whirling up and down and into the borrow pit. As Denny taxied across the highway, Earl rode across the meadow towards us on his yellow Honda 90 with a shovel bungeed across the handlebars and his hyper little black and white border collie blurring around the lush emerald grass. Earl was out opening and closing the myriad ditches that flood irrigate his hay. Denny shut the motor off just inside Earl's gate and told me that Earl might be coming to ask him to quit using his meadow now that the grass hay was up a good foot.

Earl putted up, pulled a pack of butts from his bib overalls, and asked if it was okay to smoke, as if this whole deal could just blow up anytime. He straddled his muttering scooter.

Denny said, "Hope we ain't hurting the hay crop."

"Hope my water don't mess up—what would you call it—your landing strip?" Earl replied.

"Landing strip sounds about right," Denny agreed.

Earl is a bit jaded about aviators in his hay meadow. A few years back, McCurdy, the one-eyed Vietnam vet, totaled a Cessna out here. McCurdy maintained that he was practicing a "one-wheel crosswind landing." Townsfolk, unimpressed with his euphemism, simply regarded it as a dumb plane wreck that he limped away from.

While Earl sucked on his cigarette, Denny handed me a bicycle helmet that looked like it needed an oil change. Then he pulled the canopy out of its stuff sack. He arranged the black, green, and white-striped fabric across the grass behind the machine like he was straightening out a picnic blanket ten feet wide and forty feet long. He clapped once and walked around inspecting things but looked like he couldn't find something, then shrugged and began my flight schooling. "This oughta work," he said. "You just don't know until you do it."

"On your takeoff start out slow," he said evenly as he hustled down the fabric wing, making order of the dozens of shroud lines. "Be smooth with the throttle. Get up a little speed and you'll feel the chute fill up behind you. If you remember, look over your shoulder to see if things look, uh, normal. Then goose that throttle, and stay on it and pretty soon you'll be flying. Stay on it until you clear those power lines." He pointed at the three-phase lines a quarter mile to the west that run to the ranches up Three Mile road.

"I guess we're good to go," he said.

Earl, squatting on his motor scooter, looked bemused. "You're going to fly, Harp?" he asked.

"Why not, Earl," I countered, "those dirt bikes kill more people than these things." I didn't want to start in on his cigarettes.

"Maybe so," Earl replied "But it's not as far to fall."

Earl, a Republican Powell County commissioner, remembered to show equanimity and added, "Looks fun." He smiled covertly and coughed into his fist for a couple of seconds, and said too late, "Bad boy, Bill," as his dog finished pissing on the aircraft's front tire. Bill wheeled, scratching up tufts of grass and dandelions, flinging them over the top of the Skye Ryder and on to the great, flaccid wing draped over the native hay.

Denny chuckled ruefully, gathering his thoughts for the rest of my ground schooling. He plunged into an explanation of how to land this thing. "Like I said, ease back on the throttle and you'll come down. Hell, Harp, you'll know what to do."

"How much throttle do you use when you land?" I asked.

"Oh, it's different every time. It's heating up this morning, it'll take a little more."

"Okay, how many revs on the tachometer should I be looking for?"

"You're gonna be pretty busy. Don't get hung up looking at the tach," he said. "Just come in low and slow and flare it like a parachute when you're maybe six, eight feet off the ground. If you don't like the looks of things give 'er the gas and come around for another try. Gas is cheap," he said, with a Zen-like wink.

He stuffed his hands in his pockets and looked around the meadow and said, "One more thing, there's a bunch of irrigation ditches out here." He nodded deferentially at Earl. "Why don't you circle around a little and make sure you're picking out a place to land that don't have ditches."

All this talk wasn't getting me in the air, and wouldn't matter much anyway when it came time to land. I did my first few skydives in the Soviet Union, ignorant of Russian, under the tutelage of a Red Army colonel who couldn't speak English. I figured that a million people have jumped out of airplanes and once I jumped, I'd figure out what to do next. Sergei Kiselov, the Soviet colonel who took me under his wing, so to speak, taught me a lot about trust, and it all worked out and ever since, when magazine assignments take me to Russia we still head to the aerodrome and get in a bunch of jumps together.

We looked gratuitously at the shroud lines for twists or tangles and then I settled into the seat and buckled up. Denny pulled the starter rope and the little motor stuttered alive. Denny's bicycle helmet was small, I tried without success to clinch the chinstrap. Somehow I could hear my heart thumping above all. "Why not a motorcycle helmet?"" I hollered, and tossed the helmet to Denny wondering if he could hear my heart too. Denny killed the engine and offered, "You don't gotta go up, Harp. To answer your question: weight?" he shrugged.

Before I tightened the lap belt I tossed him my Swiss Army knife and told him if anything bad happened he could keep it. He weighed my pocketknife in his hand and surveyed, perhaps for the last time, this $7,000 machine that he built from scratch and he had the heart to say, "Nice knife." I reached up to restart the motor.

Denny cleared back. Earl gunned his dirt bike and circled around well behind Denny. I pulled twice on the starter rope and the two-cycle engine burped maniacally and ranted up to speed. Bill, who had started barking at this din in the meadow, took his cue from Earl and hopped behind the Honda with his tail between his legs. The propeller behind my head pushed enough air to get the machine rolling. The ram-air canopy, which comprises a row of fabric tubes meant to capture air, were filling up and I was moving along the grassy pasture and began lifting off the ground. Air flooded into the oblong openings in the leading edge and began inflating the unfurling canopy. As my speed increased I watched over my shoulder as the big wing rose off the ground behind me like a wall. I could feel it holding me back. But as the pusher propeller increased the speed of the rollout, the fabric wall climbed and arced overhead. I looked up and saw a convincing wing. I gained speed and the ground fell away.

It was strange to feel the billowing tug of the canopy transferred through the frame and plastic seat instead of pulling at my crotch and chest as it does when I'm harnessed to a parachute. Once I was air-borne and climbing I began swinging sideways, like a pendulum, prob-ably from a little cross wind, and I thought of one-eyed McCurdy's crosswind mishap. The wing over my head tilted and undulated dra-matically from side to side. My attempts at stabilizing the canopy seemed like a second-hand experience; like I was guessing about how to fly this thing. I pressed my feet along the steering pipes, trying to control the oscillations, but the response of the big wing was practi-cally imperceptible. I scooted down in the seat to get more leverage. This canopy didn't respond at all as a sport chute does. I realized with mounting misgivings that this was truly a new experience. But with my right hand on the stubby little throttle I could ascend at will and I did. The receding ground forgotten, I was truly flying. The triangle of tubing that drew to a point beneath my feet hardly impeded my view. This was the most engaging way to fly that I could imagine. To be able to ascend while suspended under a parachute canopy was an epiphany. Instead of just descending, giving in to gravity like one does when skydiving, I felt omniscient while gaining altitude and seeing the ground drop away.

By the time I got to the power lines I was up about 150 feet. I made a wide left turn out over the couple dozen homes, two churches and store that comprise Avon proper. It seemed vaguely intrusive; flying along at no more than a leisurely bicyclist's pace, invading what little privacy such a small, tight town affords. I could see skimpy woodpiles; vehicles with their hoods open and white major appliances lying around in people's back yards. Avon looked shoddy and dangerous. I wondered where I could land if the engine quit. I flew southeast, over the corrals by the railroad siding, and still climbing out over the highway, I headed for the east end of town where the softball game was in late innings.

My wife, Lisa, was at second base. Her long-armed sister, Marta plays third. My daughter, Flannery, was playing catcher and her brother, Derry, was minding Mrs. Berg's kids. She's the pitcher and 6th through 8th grade teacher at Avon's two-room school. Denny's wife, Peggy, a true slugger, plays center field and has time to contemplate the sky and I figured she must have been wondering who was flying the Skye Ryder.

No one down on the dirt diamond knew it was me up there. I couldn't hear them for the two-stroke engine crackling behind my head as I cut back on the throttle. I flew over the ballpark at a jogger's pace about 200 feet above ground level. I was closer to home plate than the outfielders. I thought I caught a waft of Coach Kathy's cigar. They were between innings but I felt infelicitous; a distraction, and goosed the throttle, climbing east.

Seeing Avon unfold to the softball game from this limited omniscient view was glorious. For about the tenth time I thought this was the most pleasant way to fly that I could imagine.

The Little Blackfoot valley narrows down dramatically just east of the ballpark. I didn't know if the Skye Ryder would turn sharply enough to avoid the timbered slopes that form the valley's gap. Denny had mentioned that, according to my altimeter, they are 700 feet high, and my wrist altimeter showed me at 400 feet. I didn't know if I had time to climb over them. I pushed on the long pipes to which the steering toggles were fastened and, again, not feeling the response that I'd expect from a parachute, I released the throttle, reached up and grabbed the toggle-line above my right shoulder, the way I would in a parachute, pulled hard and then harder and involuntarily hollered "SHIT" at the alacrity of the canopy's response. In a hard turn you lose altitude. It was my most dramatic maneuver so far and I let go of the toggle and pushed the throttle all the way forward to regain the altitude I'd lost in the steep turn as I swept over the softball diamond, headed sort of southwest. Impressed at how well the little bugger climbed, I reached up and pulled sharply on the left steering line, laughing gratefully at discovering how to get some performance out of this machine.

Later I learned that the softball players, who have become accustomed to Denny's buddha-like silhouette under the translucent canopy, became curious about this cursing, laughing pilot with the flailing arms who circled above their game for a few minutes.

I stayed on the throttle and climbed in a lazy spiral and headed back over towards the highway above which a cumulus cloud was building. When I flew into the rising column of warm air under the cloud the whole rig bounced like I'd hit a speed bump and I was pressed down hard into the plastic bucket seat and I gained a couple hundred feet of altitude in seconds. But just as suddenly, my butt lost contact with the seat as I fell out of the rising column of warm air. I felt like a leaf above a trash fire; like things could start up that I'd have no idea how to handle. Sure enough, as I tried tugging at the great canopy, circling back over the highway, I floated back into the other side of the invisible column of rising air and began gaining altitude. My butt got pressed hard into the seat for a couple seconds. I circled around to the left, pulling the steering toggle line in a tight, satisfying, ascending bank over the Little Blackfoot and Highway 12. I'd found a thermal about the size of a basketball court and I tightened my seat belt and flew back and forth in that rising air for fifteen minutes or so. The thermal air that was rising up from the black highway was carrying me up to the cumulus cloud forming at around 6,000 feet. The air was boaty and manageable once I got comfortable with its amorphous edges. When you are rising in a fortuitous thermal, and your fabric wing flies into the edges, the downdrafts flop your wingtips like elephant ears, and you use your weight, balance, and steering toggles to stay inside the confines of the rising air. A few cars and pickup trucks and semis and a silver-roofed bus passed beneath me like swift fish in a shallow stream. I couldn't hear them from just 1,000 feet above ground level, what with an obstreperous little motor throbbing a few inches behind my head. I realized that I could ride that column of rising air right up to the base of the clouds and chickened out. I turned away to see about trying to land. When you turn out of the warm, rising air, descending cool air defines the edge of the thermal you've been using to ascend and you fall faster than you'd like. For a couple of seconds the canopy was at about level with my feet. But I got things back under control and wanted to be done with this experiment and headed back.

Back down in the meadow, Earl and Bill and Denny stood as still as cottonwood stumps. I circled about 100 feet above and gave them the old aviator's thumbs up. I circled once, and looked for the ditches that could mess up my landing. As I made another circle out over Denny's shop, his flaccid windsock told me that I could land in any direction I chose. I dove directly to the northwest, back towards Earl's hay meadow.

On my approach I had only a 60 foot tall row of cottonwoods to clear at the east end of the meadow, then I eased back to about a quarter throttle. Things looked about right. I hoped Denny took comfort hearing the smoothness of the drop in RPMs. Going easy on the throttle was the only thing happening that felt right. "This thing doesn't handle at all like a parachute," I kept telling myself.

Crossing just above the state highway and descending I had to goose it once to clear the windrow of mature cottonwoods along the eastern edge of the meadow. From about 20 feet above them I saw Earl, Bill, and Denny peripherally. I cut back on the gas, and began descending rapidly. I waited a few seconds, watching the lush green grass rising, then I reached up and pulled hard on both toggle lines to flare the canopy to land, but I let the lines go and reflexively returned the throttle to full. The two rear wheels hit and bounced me back up several feet. "I had it," I realized, as I climbed slowly, so I jerked back on the throttle, flared the canopy again and landed on the rebound. The Skye Ryder lands at 26 miles per hour, which seems real fast when your butt is six inches off the ground. But I was committed to staying on the ground and I wondered what else to do. I dug my heels into the slick grass. The Skye Ryder rolled slower. The canopy stalled and started collapsing behind me. I remembered to shut off both ignition switches, and the prop stopped as the wing sighed down behind me.

Earl pointed at me across 40 yards of his hay meadow, an indecipherable gesture, with his face obscured in the shade of his dirty cowboy hat. He and Bill wheeled around and went back to irrigating hay and harassing gophers.

Denny can't exactly sprint any more, but he kind of skipped through the dandelion-studded meadow. He stopped 10 yards short of me and looked down at the bent grass of my landing and paced off the length of the track my boot heels made in the meadow.

"Pretty good," he said breathlessly. "Sixty feet and change. Never measured it before. Man, that thing looks good in the air."

I apologized for a less than graceful landing. "Don't worry," Denny beamed, "you'll do better next time." Which was what I wanted to hear.

He told me about a guy in the Helena valley, who takes off from the street in his trailer court, and has flown more than two hundred hours on Skye Ryders and hunts coyotes from the air with a ball-joint mounted twelve-gauge shotgun. Denny thinks he could safely land a Skye Ryder on the roof of a trailer house.

"Whose trailer, yours or his?" I asked.

"Well, hell, either one, but his ain't no double-wide." Denny bragged.

The idea of this graceful, accessible form of flight, and trailer houses are intertwined. These machines, like hang gliders, paragliders, and ultra-lights, make flying egalitarian. The owners/pilots may live in trailers, but they are playful people who take to the air in machines cheaper than a used motorcycle. They don't need licenses, registration, airports, radios, or thousands of dollars worth of training. Their urge to fly is pure; they have no military or commercial designs. Some will be killed flying these things. No one could readily tally the score on gravity versus humans who would fly. That flight is possible for people like me and Denny and a coyote hunter living in the Leisure Village trailer court invests our lives with a wealth of possibilities.

It was hard to appreciate that wealth at the moment because Denny told me that he's getting a little bored with this whole deal. I was surprised because I know he wants to be a Skye Ryder sales associate.

He told me he thought it would be fun to fly places with other people, like an aerial motorcycle club. Like the four guys who landed their Skye Ryders in Avon to gas-up a while back. They were on their way from Wisconsin to Tacoma. "They thought it could take them a couple more weeks to get there. They also thought they wouldn't make it. Thing is, they didn't care." He paused. "I'd sure like to fly with somebody," he said shyly.

A white Volvo station wagon with a pair of blue kayaks strapped to the roof pulled off on the shoulder of the highway a hundred yards away. Denny admitted that he likes flying when he knows people are watching.

"Well, don't try to make it more exciting than it should be," I told him, and shook his hand for the third time since I landed. "Naw. No problem." he said, and hummed serenely as he pulled on his helmet. He sat down and belted up and yanked the starter rope and was climbing out towards the power lines in a minute.

When I got back over to the softball diamond, the victorious Avon Ladies were taking batting practice and giving some kids a turn at the plate. The softball players, who have become accustomed to Denny's serene silhouette under the translucent canopy, were curious about the cursing, laughing pilot who passed over their game for a few minutes. My son, Derry, and his pal Brett Wheeling rode up to me on their tricked-out mountain bikes.

Derry asked quietly, "Was that you in Denny's, uh, flying machine?"

Derry and Brett are learning the gravity-defying intoxication of trampolines, and I didn't want to trivialize any of this sounding hearty.

"Yeah," I said.

Brett, who can do a full flip with a half twist, said, "You flew Denny's one-seater. You flew alone?"

"It was glorious."

"Cool," they chorused, and popped wheelies over to the schoolhouse swing set that they outgrew for a couple of years until they discovered swinging as high as they can and jumping.

Last week Derry asked me, "If a guy can do a flip on the trampoline, couldn't he do one off a picnic table?"

"I suppose," I said, "but it would be different." I told him he would have to be way faster than he is on the trampoline. He'll probably try it soon.

And soon, one golden Northern Rockies evening, I'll head down to Denny's to see about my pocketknife.

Hoping the Trash Holds

(previously published in Whitefish Review, Summer 2014)

Author Note: A writer may run into material in the oddest settings.

Organisms in Petri dishes don't die from lack of nutrients. Their own waste eventually kills them. I kind of collided with the obverse side of this coin one cold January day. Whatever brinksmanship humans are facing with trashing our planet, the fat guy had landed on his own waste, which, ironically, saved him from some broken bones, or worse. From the tailgate of his idling diesel pickup to the dumpster floor had to be a twelve foot fall. His trash broke his fall.

We no longer have a dump or a landfill in Avon, Montana, a small town of 80 or so families mostly employed in extractive industries; logging and mining, ranching and maintaining a railroad that supplies 20,000 ton loads of coal to Centralia, Washington, making several runs every day through the foothills that drain west into the Little Blackfoot valley along Montana's Great Divide.

The county bulldozer pushed dirt over the old dump up Gimlet creek twenty years ago and the trash transfer station was built near the café on Highway 12. It comprises a long dirt ramp, about the size of a tilted tennis court, wide enough to make a u-turn at the top, whereupon one backs up to the edge of a foot-high concrete bumper and dumps trash into a container below that is eight feet wide, eight feet deep, and about thirty feet long. The width of the portable dumping pit allows for two drivers to back up to it and no one feels crowded. The county trucks the trash to god-knows where; we don't have to worry about throwing anything away. You see grass clippings and pruned fruit tree branches and dead dogs and all manner of offal and "Ozzie and Harriet" furniture and appliance discards in our transfer station bins. Occasionally someone will leave a stained, but still plump easy chair or couch off to the side that languishes under the rain and sun and cold nights for weeks. I think my dogs might appreciate it, but I draw some sort of line at white trashdom. Many of us refer to the local transfer station as the "Avon Mall."

Last January I noticed as I drove up the ramp someone had, rather rudely, backed sideways in their $60,000 Dodge Ram pickup towards the concrete curb, thus preventing anyone else from backing alongside to dump their load. As I low-geared up the ramp with a bag of Christmas detritus in the back of the Subaru I could see no evidence of the driver anywhere. The truck, to my annoyance, was one of those four doors with a four-foot box, nothing in which one could haul any significant load of hay or firewood. A truck that probably had a video player in the back seat. These pickup simulacrums have always put me off, and this one also had a lift kit, and fake fender extensions like high heels and shoulder pads; both costly affectations to give the driver the extra few inches of elevation and width over other, similarly useless trucks, like steroidal shopping carts. These monster trucks seem to imply that it would take five humans and four doors to deal with the cargo in the afterthought of a bed. "Okay boys, everyone grab a bale and the herd will be good," the proud owner must say, securing his wife's stabled mares for another week. You see them all over now, 7,000 pound trucks driven to pickup pizzas or haul caged dogs, or lawnmowers, with overweight humans hammering the fuel pedal to hurry up and save something, maybe time, maybe to hasten the end of nature, whatever that means. I am jaded.

I considered just driving to the café, a half-mile down Highway 12, and having a cup of coffee while this ramp hog finished his business.

It must be startling to some people when they realize, always too late, that there are other people on earth.

Compelled by the lack of evidence of anyone around, even as the Ram 3500 diesel engine idled, I got curious. I parked on the side of the ramp and walked up the packed, crunchy snow to see what the hell was going on. It was about 2 P.M., early January, the temperature was six below zero and headed south, and I wanted to get this simple chore done. As I ascended the ramp I was eye-level to the underside of the pickup and I couldn't see any legs behind it. There was no one sitting in the cab. Peering down into the all-but-empty dumpster, I saw the top of a bald human head.

I sort of whispered, "Buddy ..." for some reason. A slumped, hatless fat guy looked up, brushing off some trash bags he'd piled on himself. I stood on the lip of the dumpster and saw a 70-ish, morbidly obese man clad only in a black V-neck sweater, blue jeans and penny loafers without socks. I was damn near dumbstruck but managed to shout, "Hey, buddy, what's up?"

He sat motionless and beseeched, "Please," as he brushed off remnants of castaway trash he'd burrowed into. A pallid face, with narrow eyes and blue, putty lips intoned, "Help," which he slurred. I thought he might be drunk. I asked him if he could stand. He rolled off the trash pile over his vast torso and across his back on to his belly; one revolution carried him a good eight feet, and with an effort that was both alarming and embarrassing to watch he regained his feet. With his arms extended forward as though to present me with the evidence, he shambled to the corner of the dumpster where he had piled trash to try to climb out, which I admired as MacGyver-ish. The nearly empty metal dumpster amplified his mincing, grating little steps through the remaining few trash bags, which must have sounded hellish to him down there in his trap. "I piled all the trash I could, then just covered up in it," he lamented. I pondered his pathetic penny loafers, bemused that he'd gone out in this weather without socks. He was miming his trash piling efforts to escape in lieu of speech. Then he mumbled something about fainting and falling on his own trash as he was unloading.

"How long've you been in there?" I asked. It was like talking down to someone in a hell of their own devising.

"Lunchtime," he quivered, and added lugubriously, "I've been faint-ing lately."

The highway is a third of a mile away and there'd have been no one to hear him yelling.

An hour and a half trapped in a steel pit sided with rust and smears of suspect substances while the temperature hovered way be-low zero. The few trash bags that had been deposited contained little more than Christmas wrappings; bottles and cans and empty boxes and turkey carcasses, you could tell by how easily they slid away from his shuffling gait. He had piled some in the corner to climb on and saved some for insulation.

He lurched and clawed up onto the wee pile of his trash he'd built in the corner and extended a plump hand towards me. I knelt at the gunnels of the concrete barrier and reached down to him. There is a hinged steel plate that runs the length of the pit to prevent trash from falling between the dumpster and the concrete retaining wall and I would have to lift him clear of that obstacle. His fingernails were blue and his gelid hand had no grip to return. From my knees I extend-ed my torso and grabbed his forearm, which felt as flaccid as a half thawed salmon. I couldn't budge him. He complained that both his shoulders were "shot" and that this wasn't going to work. I grabbed his sweater. He said, "Don't pull. It's cashmere." I told him I couldn't lean any farther over and grab his belt or Levis or I'd just fall in there too.

Even though, a couple years back, a cell phone tower was built on the plateau above the local café, cell phones still don't work along that stretch of road. I told this stranger in his black hole that I need-ed to drive to a buddy's place and get a ladder and he completely freaked: crying, pleading, and tumbling off the trash pile. He threw his cell phone at the other end of his fetid steel cell. From his knees he put his hands together as if in prayer and implored me not to leave him. He was hoarse from all his unheeded yelling for help, but his voice was rising out of the dumpster with increasing power. His horror, the nightmare he'd been living for an afternoon, was peaking. No, I would not leave this guy. I couldn't tell him that the doors, at the end of the roll-on trash container, were blocked by the adjacent container.

"Okay, "I reassured him, "I'm going to get you out somehow." My couple of bags of wrappings and bottles and cans wasn't going to help. "I wish you'd thrown more trash in there, but we'll get you out." I figured I'd have to get down there and make better use of the meager castoffs, and do so quickly. I understood his panic and his slurred speech, symptoms of cyanosis, (advanced levels of freezing to death), and I knew if he wasn't already hypothermic he would be soon and then it'd be a matter of getting three hundred and fifty pounds of dead weight out of the damn container.

I lowered myself down in there with him, hanging onto the steel lip, and finally dropped about two feet. I couldn't imagine what this victim had been going through, but he must have harbored thoughts that he'd die down there. With a sense of purpose I hadn't felt until I dropped myself inside the trash trap, I silently piled the remaining bags and bits in the corner. He leaned against the cold steel wall and then he jerked away when he felt his cashmere starting to stick. At least he's still sweating, putting some heat out, I supposed, but I'd never run into cashmere and hypothermia simultaneously in my EMT days. I suggested he sit on a castoff blue plastic milk crate while I added to the unconvincing pile of plastic bags, boxes and unconsolidated trash in the corner of our trap.

He introduced himself as Sarge Dixon, and then put his elbows on his knees and his head in hands, looking at the rusted steel deck upon which his penny loafers rested. He said he was a retired Army anesthesiologist, which I thought would've been an officer but hadn't the energy to pursue his autobiography. It explained the sixty-thousand dollar toy truck, cashmere, and Gucci loafers. He said he was surprised that I was checking his pulse. I wrote his vital signs, (pulse and respiration), on his expansive forearm with a Sharpie, an old EMT habit; the subjective observations that narrate the last few minutes of demise that EMTs indelibly scrawl on the skin of the dying so the people in the E.R. have some history because the victims usually are speechless by the time they get there.

I tried to configure the trash into what I thought was a pile with some integrity. I did so making lots of eye contact with him, miming his earlier mime, watching for a sense of irony which would have drained some of the desperate drama out of what was going on.

Apropos of nothing, he told me his given name was Cecil, but he hadn't used his Christian name, he confided, since Vietnam. He added that he was on his way to Fort Harrison, the Veteran's hospital in Helena, to find out why he kept fainting. I figured if he was getting confessional that meant time was short. I addressed him as Cecil, which seemed to invigorate him. I added, "Ain't no bad weather, Cecil, just bad clothes," hoping to interject a lesson and levity at the same time, which is a pretty successful strategy with humans seemingly beyond hope, as far as I've seen. I sized him up briefly and guessed my estimate of 350 pounds was probably light.

Compassion goes a long way when people are in the shit. "You didn't ask for this," I said. "Now let's get you out of here." His head drooped and I chastened him: "Stay with me. Goddamnit"

But this feckless fool, in his seventies and penny loafers was slipping fast. "Hey!" I hollered, "No such thing as an ex-Marine, Cecil, Semper Fi." Then I explained succinctly and loudly as I thought a drill sergeant would, in that cracking steel echo chamber, that he needed to climb back up on the new trash pile I'd made and that I'd get up there with him somehow and boost him up where he could get a hold of the top of the dumpster and the concrete barrier. "Can you picture what we're about to do sir?" I demanded of him. His eyes glazed and my heart sank when he dropped to his knees. But he was just trying to crawl up the pile of trash as best he could. I abandoned the drill sergeant routine and pulled his sweater down over his horrifying plumber's butt, noticing an asymmetric mole the size of a dime, livid against an expanse of hirsute, goose-bumped ass cleavage that dampened my mood and made me wish briefly that I was simply hauling his carcass out of the dumpster, above which there is a sign that says: "No Dead Animals."

"Do yourself a favor. While you're at the Fort you should get that mole on your butt checked out." I told him, seeking a normal, kind of locker-room-advice tone of voice in my horror and revulsion. I doubted he or anyone else had ever seen the mole, so I had to say something. I was adopting the role of his healthcare advocate for the moment. It's fascinating to me to try to understand the different roles we play when faced with the uncertainty of human mortality, but I'm unaware of any accepted lexicon for guys minding each other's nether regions.

We should, but we don't. He remained silent, just pawing his way up the mound of refuse.

Hoping the trash holds, I climbed up next to him teetering and moving my feet around for some purchase, anything solid. I made a stirrup of my interlaced fingers and sort of prodded him into the corner and he bent forward and hiked up his baggy Levis and got a foot in my fireman's hands. Like a cheerleader I chanted: "SCRAMBLE, Cecil. Go Cecil, Go Cecil!" He straightened and rose up the dumpster corner slightly, trembled and groaned and just got his fingers on the edge of the concrete. "I have it," he exulted. "No, no, I lost it," he wailed. I saw all this and wished he wasn't focused on failing our first try. My shoulders burned, I was supporting most of his weight in my webbed fingers. My feet slipped and then found another toehold on the trash pile, my lower back was bent and starting to seize up, worse still, my hands were slipping apart. There was nothing left to do but stick my head up his butt, literally. None of his extremities had the wherewithal to haul his sorry ass out of that dumpster. So, with my head supporting his pelvic region somewhere, and with a hand on each of his massive buttocks, which I tried to regard as little more than porn star boobs, which is to say, hugely useless, I stood and lifted and got him up over the edge. He kicked me in the neck a couple times, then stepped on my shoulder and planted a penny loafer on my head as I went up on tiptoe feeling like I was part of a dance that elevated a nearly inert human out of an orchestra pit, (choreographers take note). He rolled over the concrete barrier and out of the damn dumpster. He was silent. It was like giving birth in reverse, like being a midwife from the outside in. All I could see was a penny loafer-shod foot dangling over the concrete bumper, pointed at the dank sky.

"Cecil?" I said. Nothing back.

I grabbed a broken broom handle and propped it into a paint can in the corner and got a foot on its end and was able, with the friction twixt my Carharrts against the frozen filth in the steel corner of the dumpster, to get a hand on the iron flap above and I got a leg up on Cecil's bare ankle and Gucci loafer dangling there and I worked my elbows around the icy flange on top of the cement lip and got myself out, grateful for the leverage on the dead weight of his lower leg and the grippable surface of the ostrich hide loafer. I wound up rolling over him; probably as close as I'll ever come to experiencing a water-bed, and I was laying right next to him wondering if my spine would feel wrecked for days. I was breathing hard, fast clouds that mingled with the steam emitting from his body; he'd been working pretty damn hard himself. I could smell wood smoke from town mixed with diesel fumes from his pickup, both aromas promising civilization, heat, and the end of Cecil's plight.

Cecil was splayed on his back in the improbably colorful, rubbish-stained, packed snow. Propping myself on an elbow, I shook his mushy shoulder, and said something about getting him in the truck. He opened his eyes, took a deep breath and gave me a look of astonishment, and then rolled over and we crawled. I opened the driver's door and he spent a couple minutes heaving his considerable bulk up into the cab as I brushed snow off his black cashmere back, precancerous ass crack, and piano legs. I slapped the snow off him with a pair of gloves I held in my left hand, like an old time dueling slap, sort of a purge after having had my head and hands so uncomfortably involved with his generous flesh. His engine had been idling the whole time and it felt like the extravagant heat escaping a rich guy's house as he stands in his door, not a thought of inviting you in.

According to local legend, Malcolm Forbes, the billionaire gadfly, wrecked his BMW motorcycle up by Glacier Park and he bought his first responder a similar 18 thousand dollar motorcycle. There's a story about Bill Gates getting a flat tire on the way to his ski lodge near Bozeman. A local cowboy stopped and changed his tire and Gates bought him a brand new diesel pickup.

Cecil had a way of giving away nothing. I tried to say innocuous things before I shut his door, like, "Awkward way to meet somebody, Cecil." Or, "I always wondered what'd happen if someone fell in there, with so few people who use this place." He was safe and silent, back in his pristine luxury truck, its heater nearly soundless. If he was hearing me, he had nothing to say.

While I climbed in the passenger door I wondered why a fat guy would go to the expense of making it more difficult to get into his truck by adding the lift kit. It was about 100 degrees warmer in the pickup cab and as he warmed up he finally spoke lucidly: "You saved my life." The slur was gone, he spoke very little, but he was regaining coherency. I grabbed his wrist; it was sewer pipe thick but I found his radial pulse. About 90, not scary high.

He looked sideways, not in the eye, "The Lord sent you," he declared. I wondered if I had a potential eternal gratitude slave here, but he resolved that issue as he warmed up more, chanting, "Thank you Jesus for sending this Samaritan. Thank you Jesus for sending this Samaritan," a few times.

We agreed we'd just idle down to the café, which was vacant in mid-afternoon. We sat at a four-top table next to the window nearest the parking lot. I checked his radial pulse again. Nicole, the waitress, set ice water on the table. The Army anesthesiologist got up and went to the restroom and came back and made sure I could see the cyanosis was gone. I pinched his fingernails and they went from white to pink just like you hope. His pupils were reacting to light changes evenly, his lips were pink and his eyes darted around as though he couldn't believe he was still alive.

I checked his pulse again. Then he washed down cherry pie with a latte. "I think you're gonna make it Cecil," I said. Seemingly still caring for him, I added: "You oughta go easy on the calories." I was thinking about his penny loafer on my head digging that little button on the top of my hat into my skull. I don't want to give diabetes some sort of foothold.

Doctors, perhaps anesthesiologists in particular, seem to have very little training in nutrition.

"Free country," he said with his mouth full, and nodded and clicked his fingers to Nicole and ordered another latte. He told me, "You saved Sarge's life. You …"

I interrupted, "Cecil …"

He interrupted, "Cecil would not have made it out of that shit hole." He asked Nicole to make him a latte to go.

He asked me to quit calling him Cecil and looked back in the direction of the dumpster, then towards the kitchen, and then decided: "God sent you." His dogma seemed to warm up in proportion to his core temperature.

"I have something to do. The Lord saved me because he wants

me to do something." Then he said he'd just wrecked his old Chevy pickup yesterday. "Things aren't good. But for some reason it's hard to kill old Sarge."

Cecil was dead.

He never asked my name.

"Whatever, bro, please get that mole on your ass diagnosed. Okay?"

He said he was going to head to the VA hospital. I offered to drive him. "Logistical nightmare," he said dismissively, and stood. "God bless you," he uttered in a sepulchral tone that made me think he wasn't long for this world and intuited as much. I asked if there was someone we could call who could ride this out with him. "Just moved here, down by the old Dana ranch, there's no one," he said. And awash in some reverie, he abruptly walked out, watching his loafers move across the icy parking lot with the mincing grace extra large guys can affect. He ascended into his big red Ram and drove east. Whatever old Sarge was meant to do, it didn't include picking up the check. I paid and left Nicole a hefty tip thinking ruefully of the derivation of the word "stiffed" as I walked back to the dump to retrieve my car.

I did, however, receive a gift from Sarge. He helped reaffirm my notions that religious fervor is a lousy substitute for, perhaps even obviates, common decency.

I didn't exactly save Sarge, his salvation derived from landing on a pile of his own trash. I was honored to be a coincidental stranger, and to have witnessed whatever strength he summoned as he briefly revisited being Cecil, his pre-Vietnam persona. He came real close to ending up a stiff in a dumpster. Be aware: epiphanies are ephemeral; their import, their entirety often eludes us. On the upside they can change us for good.

I related all this to my arborist partner, Fred Haefele, who, for 35 years, has saved more folks' bacon taking down hazardous trees around Missoula and Helena than any one. Fred is a fit, fearless, tree-climbing senior, has written three books, has one Triumph motorcycle, two stents, and two teenagers and an understanding of more knots and knotty relationships than any sailor. A couple days later, doing windshield time under a load of spruce limbs we were hauling to the Helena dump, I mused about whether the guy would ever try to find out who saved him from his dumpster, maybe call and invite me out for a recip-rocal lunch or piece of pie. "You'll never get a bowl of bullion out of that nimrod. That 'God saved me, God sent you' stuff marginalized you." Fred has taught hundreds of people to become better writers at Stanford and Missoula and through workshops that supplement his in-come as an arborist and writer. He knew I felt dissed but Fred released me with a simple quote from the Beatles: "Let it be."

Treed

(previously published by Faber and Faber, *First Fictions*, London, 1988)

Author Note: An autobiographical piece I wrote while studying writing in Galway, in 1986.

In 1972, my cousin Gus and I were horse logging in the Oregon Coast Range, using a mismatched team of draft horses comprising Carbon, a compact, explosive Percheron stud, and Buck, a leggy, feckless, Shire-cross gelding, to skid our sawlogs to the roadside. We had slogged around in the cold mud all winter, earning a hundred bucks a day apiece every day we managed to get sixty logs to the landing. It was hard work for damn good money. We often took no more comfort on those cold days than sliding our bare hands between the horse's steaming shoulders and their smooth, sodden collar pads to thaw our fingers. Spring had come early. By mid-May we were into longer arid days that had us starting at 5:30 A.M. so we could quit early, before the woods turned hot with the portentous buzzing that might be insects, or might be something worse building up. We worked spooked, as though differential equations that we couldn't grasp were adding up to big bad news.

During the week we overnighted the horses up at the job site in a small corral of poles spiked to trees in a rectangle with a crude tin shed roof at one end that drained into a clawfoot tub for their water.

Every weeknight either Gus or I would stay in a wall tent at the job site, while the other guy went back home to shower and feed the chickens and goats and rest up. Some nights in the hasty forest corrals the horses would stomp and snort and whinny at such length I wondered how they got by on so little sleep. We were careful about our food, suspending it between trees, out of the reach of bears. But twice, the horse's plastic grain can that we held shut with a bungee cord had been dragged away by a bear a few feet into the woods and broken open.

At first, I slept with a few railroad flares at hand. Then I got a big-bore pawnshop six-shooter to defend myself if a bear came prowling in the tent. Gus wouldn't hear of having a gun around. What good would it do? Waking up myopically, with a bear a couple feet away and firing blindly at the blackness. One shot that didn't drop the bear instantly would only bring on an ugly, mortal struggle. Gus derided my handgun and kept a sharp, sheathed knife under his pillow so he could slice his way out of the tent. The odor of gunpowder troubled Gus's head.

The damn bears were the least frequent of my worries. Gus and I both believed that Buck might kill one of us some day, pulling a log over our skinny chests when we fell on the skid trail, or with an unpredictable kick from one of his Frisbee-sized hooves. We had a pact that the survivor wouldn't shoot him in revenge and leave him for the bears, birds and coyotes, but sell him to a cannery, assuring his future as a ton of scattered poodle turds in Portland.

I also believed that Gus might kill me some day. He'd been back from Vietnam less than two years and he was haunted and seemed to get lost in thoughts that made him wince quickly or just check out completely for minutes at a time. Those lapses could be deadly on a logging job. We were cutting down eight-story-tall fir trees and using one-ton horses to pull forty-foot logs down steep slopes where knee-high undergrowth demanded fast feet.

"Man, this is how it felt," Gus would say, as we stood in a fog on a densely timbered mountainside with a driving rain dinging our hard-hats. I'd think: "Goodbye," and Gus would lose himself in a reverie that made him real twitchy for quite a while. We had a lot of foggy days.

One morning, as we were walking the team into a job, somebody nearby took a few potshots with a small bore gun. Gus jumped behind a stump, went fetal, and called in an air strike on our position while miming a radio transceiver against his ear. While he ducked behind the stump I shouted at the unseen shooter to get the hell out of here, tied the horses to some brush and grained them, filed our chainsaw, and ate a sandwich.

Gus never told me to take cover with him.

"That's the way it started," he said, when he shook it off half an hour later. "Small arms. A few shots. Then the shit storm, a mad minute at a time." He was not yet making eye contact.

That feeling of being bulletproof that young men must own when they are learning to be warriors or bubbas or salesmen had been stolen from Gus in Vietnam. Now I thought Gus had taken all that away from me. My resentment of his VFW solipsism was eating me up. I wanted my hubris back. I'd more or less promised my aunt that I'd try to keep her crazed young veteran of war, who we hardly knew anymore, out of trouble. But I was afraid of his lapses and hardened to his anger and I had no faith that my amateur psychology was up to the challenges.

His dad, my dad's brother, was an adored old pillar of family medicine in Portland, and his mom was the most compassionate volunteer social worker in town. His folks had helped raise me through a couple of rocky years after my father died young. For two years I'd spent most of my spare time in my uncle's study, reading the encyclopedia.

Most of Gus's ten siblings were getting to be success stories. The comparisons were inevitable. Since his discharge, Gus had quit premed school, married and divorced, and wrecked a car and a motorcycle while drunk. He was tall and skinny and wore army issue wire-rimmed eyeglasses, never shaved his chin whiskers or cut his hair, drank heavily and pissed off a lot of people in town with his balls-to-the-wall disregard for even the few proprieties that are observed in loggers' bars. He took up with tattooed women and treated them with the same rough regard he had for horses. Most of his real self-destructive stuff had abated when we began putting the horse logging business together, but I was ready to bail out, growing less concerned every day with how he'd plummet without someone to keep him afloat.

One Friday afternoon, after coaxing and leading Buck and Carbon into the back of the stock truck to haul them home for the weekend, I proposed a plan that I thought would buy me some time away from him.

"You want to haul these guys home and unload them, Gus?"

"No," he answered. "Why?"

He had never driven the stock truck because neither of us trusted him to.

"All you need to remember is to keep it in second gear all the way down the mountain, and telegraph the horses with a little fake turn before every curve, and tap the brakes for them, so they brace themselves before you really stop," I said, wondering if this solo drive would mean the end of the whole operation and thinking that would work out okay somehow.

"Staying here to commune with nature?" he asked.

"I'm going to walk over and see how Bruno's doing," I said. Bruno Andare, a middle-aged logger, was "pioneering" a road into a section he was going to start "selectively cutting" on the other side of the range, on the Luckiamute river, which was two drainages and about a six mile walk due north.

Bruno's notion of selective cutting was to select a mountain and cut all the trees. I told Gus I was a little concerned about Bruno as this was his first logging job since he'd had a heart attack a few months ago. I also intended to have a word with him about sustainable forest management practices that I'd been reading up on, that some heavy equipment operators were experimenting with.

Gus and I had a fondness for Bruno that derived partly from a ride home from our favorite bar, the Logger's Rest, one night the winter before. Deputy Dale, the local lawman, had pulled us over at about 2:00 A.M. Bruno, in the driver's seat, slurred his lines to the deputy. Dale told him to get out of the pickup and walk along the white line at the edge of the pavement. Bruno was five foot six or seven and weighed about 125 pounds and flat-topped his black hair like a pool table brush. Pure heart and willingness had propelled him through thirty years of logging. That's probably why someone so disproportionate to his chosen profession and seemingly fit could have his heart try to opt out early.

Bruno squatted with his head between his legs astride the white stripe and then raised himself up, legs kicking at the crescent moon, and he walked that line on his hands. Spare change spilled out around his flat palms onto the damp pavement. Bruno walked on his hands, stepping daintily around the twirling coins in the headlight wash, and he kept walking. Dale duckwalked alongside like he was inspecting Bruno's manicure, then stood up and straightened his tie. Bruno, back on his feet, staggered noticeably, ignored his coins, and climbed back in the pickup.

"You dumb ape, get the hell home," Deputy Dale said.

But Gus and Bruno's connection ran deeper than that. Bruno was a veteran of the war in Korea, and he and Gus, warily at first, then wearily, acknowledged their shared coming-of-age serving-their-country deals. Bruno and Gus had taken to hanging around his pickup of an evening each with a muddy pants leg propped on the back bumper and killing a six-pack while lounging over Bruno's truck box telling each other war stories. They looked down at broken chokers, spilled corn, oats and barley, chainsaws, fuel cans, and wedges and lying in the film of oil and grit in the truck bed and they spoke of Asian places where they'd both seen deaths and caused deaths. They spoke fondly, in the jargon of parts numbers and acronyms for gear they had used. They affected to laugh at death; theirs, anybody's. I envied that camaraderie.

Back at our logging show, Gus begrudgingly agreed to drive the team home, which meant he'd also have to unload, unharness, curry, and feed them. I quashed a pang of gratitude and reminded him: "Second gear. Telegraph the horses," and headed north afoot.

It was a four hour walk across the top of Bonner Ridge and down to where Bruno was working. I carried nothing, but had only to reach out for ripe salmonberries and blackberries to slake my thirst and keep my blood sugar up. I thought about the stories I'd heard from older loggers about Bigfoot encounters. We all believed that in this enriched environment, this incredibly edible landscape, why wouldn't there be some elusive primates making an invisible, honest living off this country.

The orange and purple juice from the berries mixed and stained the black creases in my hands blood red. I rolled the berries around in my mouth like wee beads of warm wine and juice leaked down my chin.

The blood-red juice on my hands looked like some sanguine proof of survival on a planet that scratched and clawed but rewarded deft plucks between the thorns.

I left my moustache and chin stained and sticky; it seemed like a delicious infraction of rules that I didn't subscribe to, that were somehow necessary to getting along in the world. I wondered how long I'd let myself look so childish. I wondered if Gus got this little thrill magnified many times when he cussed in front of someone's wife or spit snoose on the barroom floor. His whole persona in places we went to socialize suggested a simmering willingness to fight, and probably fight dirty. His act was so obviously an act that guys backed away from him with impunity; they were leaving a mentally ill guy, a crazy veteran, alone. Nothing ignoble in that. But Gus was misreading this stuff and getting bolder.

I was striding, thinking about all this to the internal beat of the 1812 Overture, or maybe it was the theme to the Lone Ranger, they sound a lot alike, but it was marching music. My boots clumping down the road made it sound as though it were hollow. All roads have a hollow sound to them, if that's how you interpret the sound of boot soles and bones resonating with what's underfoot. Gus believed that he heard hollow sounds even in the duff of the forest floor, as though there were old bunkers down there.

He told me once that he went into the woods every morning with a feeling that he could die that day. It was the worst kind of fear, unspecific and chronic, maybe even pathological. It wasn't the tacit threat that Buck might kick him in the head, or that the last thing he'd ever feel would be the enormous crushing weight of a tree grinding him into the ground. He believed that up there in the lush fog and Coast Range drizzle some kind of whisper would kill him because of some shit he'd done overseas that he'd never paid for. But he kept going back. Either he wasn't completely absorbed by his demons or he looked forward to the axe falling.

I walked with the sun at my back. An onshore breeze from a couple miles away carried ocean smells up into the Coast range. Thorny tendrils of blackberry bushes snaked into the disused logging road and snagged my shirtsleeves, and clawed harmlessly across my waxed canvas pants. I kept to the grassy center and couldn't hear my own footfall for my whistling. I'd replaced the martial music in my head and counted cadence to Carole King's tune, "I Feel The Earth Move."

I came across a glistening bear turd and twigged through it, finding berry seeds and the pulpy purple hulls of a thousand half-digested ants. It stank of its passage through those bear innards and bear gall. My knuckles brushed it. It was still putting out heat. It was warmer than the sun-washed grey gravel it sat on. I dropped the twig and thought that even if it's true that the unexamined life isn't worth living, inspecting things too closely can give you more information than you need to get on with things.

You'd think an ursaphobe would have climbed a tree right then. But, after about a five-mile walk on a hot afternoon, I got caught up inveighing against the guys who, I'd heard, were hunting black bears just to cut their gall bladders out. In this country, the gall bladder is a reviled organ, but in Asia, it is an aphrodisiac. I'd heard that black bear gall bladders fetch $10,000 in Korea.

Once I helped my cousin Vern gut and skin a black bear that he wanted to eat. Skinned, it looked eerily human, and its internal organs were arranged exactly as ours are. Vern was very careful to tie off the gall bladder, a yellow-gray sack that could hold two golf balls, at both ends before he cut it out, so that he could sell it to some guy who dealt in such offal.

I walked along wondering how the hell someone in Asia decided that a black bear gall bladder could help his sex life, but I couldn't get past the stink of spilled gall. Some Westerners have considered that a stinking mess might help explain why our cultures clashed mortally in three 20th century wars.

Daydreaming on bears and Asia and conflicts I crested a ridge into the Luckiamute drainage and came to the freshly exposed dirt that Bruno had been flattening into a 28 foot wide road up a half-mile wide valley that was ripe for a logger's living. He'd cut the road right through the interface between the 20 to 30 inch diameter Douglas firs on the upslope and the alder creeping up from the moist ground creekside. I laid Vibram footprints on top of his zippered Cat tracks. My nose filled with the redolence of busted sod that smells like old folding money to a logger.

I descended the virgin dirt road into the valley that Bruno was fixing to log off. Douglas firs and mottled-bark alders rose up out of a mass of ferny undercover that competed for the sidelong sunlight cutting between tree stems. It was oddly quiet for one of Bruno's shows. He always worked as long as there was daylight to burn, never wasting an evening like this. "When you fall, fall in the direction of your work," was one of Bruno's mottos. I had the unsettling thought that my excuse to my cousin, about Bruno with his questionable heart, working alone, might be coming true. I wondered if I'd find him slumped on his Cat with its diesel engine ticking and cooling.

I proceeded a few hundred yards up the roughed-in road with concern creeping up and my footfall quiet in the exposed clay and my mouth slightly ajar so I could hear better. With a little letdown of relief, I heard Bruno shouldering and kicking his way up through the alder-canopied thicket below the road.

"Now what the hell is he doing down in that alder patch," I wondered. I couldn't reconcile taking alder, it's a weed tree they all said, not really worth cutting for the kind of money the paper mills are paying. But more importantly, it's a nitrogen-fixing species that loggers should leave intact to ensure healthy soil microbiology in the woods. I thought I'd try to dissuade him from cutting and wasting the alder. I figured that startling him might give me a leg up on the old fart and maybe I could begin reasoning with him, then, to leave the creekside ecosystem intact. He was the kind of guy who loves a prank, and I was seeing some possibilities.

I sidestepped back and forth at the road's edge listening to his racket as he bulled his way up through the thick undergrowth. I couldn't see five feet into the mass of vegetation as he crackled up through the salal, sword fern, viney maple, and alder garden below me. Finally, it became obvious that he would emerge from the brush at a point at my feet. He sounded about ten feet down in there as I leaned over the edge of the road to stick my hand in his face as he emerged from the thicket.

Well, it wasn't Bruno.

Every time I've told this story that bear gets bigger. That's the way bear-encounter stories work. By now I can't keep a straight face and say his size; but this was definitely a black bear, somewhere between the size of a Volkswagen and the largest carnivore you'd ever want to have show up between your outstretched hand and your face.

His bloody muzzle and the sickly-sweet moldy smell of him are forever imprinted on my brain. Bears pick up a few scars along the way, and he appeared to have just won a fight. His momentum carried him right up on the road into my torso and he spun me around, nearly knocking me down. We both bellowed.

If I had a tail it would have preceded me as I sprinted down the road, my pathetically short life seeming vulnerable. I could see my body, gutted, torn, already turning to bear turds. But horse logging builds up some pretty well-developed adrenal glands and now the old fight-or-flight instincts were all fueled up and in a full flight frame of mind and muscle. The roots of every hair on my body seemed to fizz. The wind in my armpits was leaving a trail of fear in my wake that, I was sure, would only egg the bear on.

I saw an alder limb hanging about ten feet above the road and leaped for it, thinking that the last thing I'd ever feel as I grabbed at it was a claw hooking my butt and dragging me into a set of gnashing choppers. I caught the slender limb with both hands but was almost dumped back down on the road when the tree bent under my load and then whipped back upright. As I was vaulted upwards I locked my legs around the trunk, crushing my balls insufferably, but I started shinnying up, grabbing desperately at higher limbs until the canopy forked into branches too small to support my weight. I'd cut both elbows scrambling up the tree and left a trail of blood on the rough black and white bark. As I reached down to massage my mashed crotch, I felt my red-handled pocketknife and pulled it out and opened the big blade, three inches of stainless steel that stood between me and annihilation. I pulled my chainsaw wrench out of my back pocket and laced my legs through some limbs and hung by my knees, upside down in the branches, armed and listening.

Upside down, I figured I was about ten feet up the tree. The bear would have to climb some to get me, he wouldn't be able to just grab a foot and haul me down. I couldn't see much what with the leafy canopy from which I had dangled my body, but I listened intensely through labored breathing and the blood pumping through ears and my brain as I hung there looking at Bruno's road above my head, so to speak, ready to start stabbing.

The inverted universe outside my tree, which fluttered softly with my jiggling, was silent, as though the whole neighborhood understood that the stalk was on, the demise of a logger was imminent, and they couldn't wait for the death throes to begin.

I wished that the fight would get started. I didn't think I could hold out much longer capsized, with aching balls, red rivulets tracing both arms, and my head filling with my remaining blood. I couldn't hear a thing. He was waiting with the silent patience of all predators, not wasting energy, knowing he had me treed.

Then I heard him padding softly down the road. He made a weird and terrible sound, almost like a human chortle. I couldn't see him, but knew he was following my spoor of fear and blood.

Well, it was Bruno.

"Who's in there? You scream like a kid."

"It's me, Harp," I whispered. "Look out, there's a bear around here."

Bruno's chortle unstrangled itself into an outright laugh.

Truth be known, I wasn't ten feet up that tree. My eyes weren't much farther above Bruno's than when we're both on our feet.

He said, "Lord," kind of startled, when he first saw me hanging there. Then he fell over laughing. He began choking and clutching at his shirt. With mixed emotions I'd watched him lose his balance and fall to his knees, a little worried about his heart.

"Your bear was about a year-old cub that just run past me." Bruno said between wheezes. He was kneeling in the soft dirt and sizing me up from down there. "Would you put your weapons up and get down outta there, I don't want to damage the hardwoods on this piece."

"All right," I thought.

Bruno got up. I got down and surveyed the damage. I've scraped myself up worse in an average day of timber falling, but I felt that this was a more remarkable trauma, more vivid and dramatic.

Bruno and I were standing on his road now, but on totally different levels. "Poor little thing," he said, looking back up the road. "Just trying to gorge on berries."

"There was a cub too?" I asked hopefully, still trying to convince myself that I had been in some real trouble.

"What'd you do to him?" Bruno asked incredulously, "He was about the size of a fuckin' hog."

It all hit me at once. I sulked and turned my back on him like a rented mule.

"Okay, okay, let's go drown your fear," he offered.

We drove down to the river road, where the valley straightens out and widens into the shamefully sod bound former hayfield at Orval Liturgski's place. Folks overlooked Orval's neglect because he was missing quite a few fingers. As we cruised with our backs to the setting sun Bruno told me a story about Orval, whose pet pig was dozing bloated and pink in the twilight on his front porch.

"Old Orval hunted bears with dogs for years," Bruno told me. "About ten years back, Orval got tired of walking up under bears treed above his baying hounds and then shooting them pretty much point blank. He decided it would be more sporting to shoot the limb out from under an old boar up a grouse ladder fir. He put a couple rounds into the thick of the limb and it started to give, Orval was beginning to wonder what might transpire when that bear fell in amongst his dogs. Then the limb swung like a grandfather clock and dumped that bear right on Orval." Bruno was definitely rooting for the bear. "The bear, three dogs, and Orval all rolled down the hill in a hell of a mess together. There's no quit in them dogs. Dogs don't think about just letting the damn bear amble off." It would have been the worst kind of fight: two arms and about fifteen legs all scratching and gouging, and teeth sinking into meat and bone. No gettin' out of that kind of a fight until there's no chance of any more fighting.

"Orval lost three fingers, one at a time, but doesn't know who to," Bruno regaled me as the story elevated me from my own travails. "That bear kicked ass, and then hauled ass," he said gleefully. "Orval had to shoot two of those dogs; too chewed up to save, and he had to do it without his regular trigger finger." He sniffed, laughed, and coughed and cleared his throat.

"Then," Bruno continued, "Orval took his last bear hound to the veterinarian and traded him in exchange for having his stumps sewn up and that was the end of his bear hunts." I thought Orval was missing more than three fingers, but Bruno cut the story off as he turned on to the paved county road.

About a mile down the road the Logger's Rest neon was blinking on. My red stock truck sat in the pastel glow like a slat-sided cube perched behind the curvaceous 1949 International cab. No horse heads sticking up out of it.

"Shit, my cousin's there," I said, my anxiety spilling out on the seat between us.

Bruno looked at me twice and said "I'll shut up about how you can scare a knee-high bear cub into a dead run while climbing a sapling ...."

"Yeah. Shut up," I interrupted.

He reeled back darkly and said, "Lighten up."

He slowed the truck and pulled off the road a couple hundred yards from the bar.

"Goddamit," I said, "I thought I was going to die." Bruno saw me shudder.

"You're treed all right," he said. "You're trying too hard to keep your hands in your pockets. Sometimes you gotta quit being so goddamn nervous and just look around." He picked up his thermos, shook it, and set it down slowly.

"Today you got a glimpse," Bruno said like he was haunted, and he switched the engine off.

He sat there thinking. After a long pause he shook himself and said, "A counterfeit little glimpse... get a grip." Bruno sighed wearily. "Now Orval got a good feel for bear. But when he told me that story, he said the shit he seen in the foxholes and trenches on Iwo Jima in '45 was way worse than when somebody shot his first fuckin' finger off over there." He added, "Your bear wasn't much, Harp. Cut the world some slack."

Bruno allowed that I was pretty wound up, still riding the wave of adrenaline that had launched me into the alder sapling. "Now Gus," he said, and cleared his throat. "Take what you felt for a couple minutes and imagine living like that every day, all day and all night for a year, like Gus did. He had no way out of Vietnam early but feet first. You don't come down off that kind of a high, even if you want to, for years, if ever."

"Headcase," I said.

"Prime case," Bruno agreed. "What the hell," he shrugged. "We're all freaks."

He looked at me for agreement and I felt privileged to be included in his world. He perked up as I dropped my sull.

"Vets," he said sadly. "Most of them eventually get better. The losers were probably coming unscrewed before Uncle Sam got ahold of them. Your cousin? Who the fuck knows? He's on the edge. You guys were raised right. That might be the difference. Hang in there." He reached over and patted my suspender with the back of his hand. Then he pulled his hand back quickly and took his hard hat off and gave his black crew cut a scratching. "What are you guys, about twenty two? What the fuck else you going to do? Fatten up some nice chick on a shoe salesman's salary?"

He slipped his pickup into neutral and we coasted the rest of the way down to the Logger's Rest. Through the front window we could see Gus sucking on a bottle of Rainier, ignoring Orval, the only other patron in the place. I shambled in with Bruno, experimenting with a bowlegged stride that attempted to give my sore balls some space.

Gus looked up at the two of us, noted the blood on my arms, and, I suppose, the oxblood berry juice down the front of me. His eyebrows arched quizzically.

"Treed," I responded. "Several black bears," I said, and gave Bruno a menacing look. "Bruno scared them off," I added with an ambivalent little nod of gratitude.

Bruno nodded back, straight faced.

"Far out," Gus said.

Orval, who was 70, but looked about 90, was sitting a couple stools down from Gus, rolling a cigarette somehow with his stumps. He cranked his saggy face sideways and said, "Tough guy," over his shoulder at Bruno.

Bruno thumped Orval on the back and Orval dropped his roll-yer-own on the bar. Gus watched all this intently, his aloofness forsaken. I watched Gus, but couldn't tell if he was looking to see a little hassle start up or if he was curious about this kind of friendship between a couple of guys.

Orval licked his stumps. He daintily lifted the yellow paper, with its tobacco furrow slightly scattered along the factory crease. In one deft motion he rolled it, inserted in his mouth, withdrew it with a twist, and held it in his truncated old paw in front of his nose, gazing at it cross-eyed and content.

"Far out," Gus said warmly. "You got some feeling through all those scars?"

"Enough," Orval said.

Choking Near to Death: the Auto-Heimlich

(previously published by the Helena Independent Record)

Author Note: A much shorter version of this piece was carried in the local newspaper as a P.S.A.

I went to swallow some vitamins a couple days ago that I had thrown into a sandwich bag with some chocolate covered espresso beans. I'd left the little package in my pickup and the capsules and candy had melted together. I broke off a chunk that seemed to have about the right number of pills and chocolate-coated beans and, as always, had a pint glass of water to wash the everything down. I should have chewed it a little, but I regard as kind of cool my ability to throw a dozen vitamins in my maw and flush them down easily. But what I popped in my mouth was a wad, not a handful, of unconsolidated pills. The coalesced mass of pills and candy, roughly the size of a golf ball, went down the wrong pipe and my first startled inhalation probably lodged it more firmly in my trachea, the tube that carries air to your lungs. That was the last breath I drew for a while, and could have been the last one ever.

For reasons unknown to me still, except that I was panicked, I kind of loped around the central chimney in my house, covering, perhaps, four laps, while trying to retch. Finally, convinced that I'd fall over dead pretty soon because I hadn't taken a breath during these exertions, I quit running around. Back in my kitchen, my dog Max, who'd never seen such shenanigans, had been trotting alongside me barking. I tried to shush him and realized that I couldn't manage a whisper. I ended up at the sink, certain that I had just a few seconds left before I passed out and then died. I balled up my fist and laid it on the edge of the kitchen counter with my thumb on top, and balled up my other fist and set it in the notch below the breastbone where the ribs fall away from each other, and I dropped onto it. Dropping didn't work. I needed to make the air left in my lungs compress explosively and dislodge the wad. I plunged desperately onto both fists, stacked up on the counter, and the clod of chocolate and vitamin capsules popped out of me, hit the window, and thunked on the sink bottom, impressing me with its solidarity. It was slimy brown; the chocolate coating looked shiny from melting slightly while it resided in my windpipe. My throat was so sore I wasn't sure for a while if I'd gotten it all out. I knew with utter certainty that I had been just seconds away from death. Survivor's euphoria hadn't kicked in yet and I felt about as alarmed as the time I had a malfunction on my main parachute. I was falling 1,000 feet every six seconds and had to cut away the main chute and pull my reserve. When I was about 800 feet above the ground I saved my own ass with two seconds to spare.

The whole incident happened in roughly 60 seconds. There was absolutely no time to seek help. I spent many years as a volunteer EMT, but I had never considered Heimliching myself. Please, dear readers, practice this. Try that move right now. Ball up your fist and place it beneath the center of your ribs. Keep your elbows tucked in so they don't spread the weight along your lower ribs. Push up and in and feel your diaphragm. Even a little push will make you expel some air. Then try stacking your fists on a counter top or chair back and see how it feels to really make some air move. That action, multiplied by adrenaline and desperation, should keep you from choking to death if you're alone. And, of course, practice doing the Heimlich on another human.

I did it once, (nominally trained in the exigencies of the procedure), in a breakfast joint in Bend, Oregon, renowned for its huge platters of food. A corpulent fellow stood up near me and was clutching his throat and obviously needed the maneuver. I approached him from behind and told him I was going to help him. I asked him to bend forward slightly and I was able to stretch my arms around his ample girth and find the spot and gave him a hard thrust at the diaphragm. A piece of sausage about the size of half a bratwurst popped out accompanied with some gastric fluids and skidded and bounced across a table where a family of four blonde people were breakfasting, whereupon they stood and marched out of the restaurant while experimenting with various manifestations of being grossed out. A young waitress walked up to me and I thought she was going to thank me for saving this glutton who had sat back down lugubriously eyeing his half empty plate. She said, "Mister, next time aim 'em at a wall or door or someplace … Jeez." My XXXL patient looked at the remains of his breakfast and bemoaned, "My throat's too sore to finish." I didn't buy his breakfast but, to placate the stiffed waitress, I bought the blonde family's unfinished eats and left a big tip.

Shaken and chastened, I could finally empathize with the big chowhound's sore throat lament. I beheld the deadly chocolate wad in the sink and paced around and composed myself somewhat and thought about the irony of dying from swilling candy and vitamins. Then I thought about not being more involved in the world around me. So I began writing this monograph, this caveat, and quick lesson.

Then the phone rang and my musical pal Bruce Anfinson, who spends his winters entertaining guests at Lone Mountain and minding his team of grade Belgian geldings, asked if I wanted to come by and sing and play some tunes. He noted the rasp in my voice and asked what's up. I told him what I'd just gone through and then I heeded his suggestion: "Well hell, Harp," Bruce said, "If you just saved your life take yourself out for a beer."

The Gall Bladder of That Man

(previously published in the King County Medical Society Bulletin)

Author Note: I regarded this essay as a P.S.A.

A few weeks ago, for the second time in as many months, I had an "intractable" pain in the upper right quadrant of my abdomen. Up there where the liver resides, just behind my lowest rib and to the right of my sternum. I'd spent three hours sitting, pacing, cursing, kneeling, curled in a fetal position; nothing helped. Since this was the second attack, I would do as I had promised myself, and head to the hospital.

I rode out the first episode at home because we don't have medical insurance. I'm a freelance writer, my wife is a potter and homemaker, and we make a decent living, but roughly 45 percent of what we earn already goes to taxes and insurance. Dishing out $600-800 dollars per month on medical insurance payments for our family of four has been no more possible for us than leasing a Mercedes Benz. We've been uninsured since we returned from two years in Ireland, in 1988, a "developing" country where medical care is free.

None of us have ever been to a hospital sick, in fact, we've never had a family doctor because we've never needed one. I have been patched up in emergency rooms for job related traumas. My daughter,

Flannery, got a concussion in a high school basketball game her junior year that cost 850 bucks. We'd been paying some kind of insurance for her for three years, through her school, but found out that we weren't covered for sports. Once, during my eight years as a volunteer emergency medical technician, a patient in an ambulance broke my thumb as I suctioned blood from what was left of his airway after a head-on collision down on Highway 12, one of Montana's deadliest roads. I was trying to keep him from drowning in his own blood and with the strength of a drowning man he reached up, grabbed my thumb, and broke it. Another time, as I put out a fire on a truckload of PVC pipe in the parking lot of the local cafe, I sucked in the fumes of the burning plastic. Later that day Lisa, my wife, returned home and found me on the front porch on my knees, nearly unable to breathe. We headed for the hospital and follow-up respiratory treatments that added up to a little more than $2,000.

That broken thumb and insulted lungs cost me dearly. Our volunteer fire department had no insurance either. I learned from those deals, perhaps insufficiently, that doctor and hospital bills seem to add up in increments of a thousand bucks.

It is said that medical bills are the biggest single cause of personal bankruptcy in the U.S. Driving into Helena with this encompassing, undiagnosed pain in my gut, I considered the fact that we could lose our home of eighteen years over what was happening to me. I wondered if I was somehow going to drown.

Lisa had been busy making pots and she told me to do the 37 mile drive to the hospital in Helena myself. She said I should take our 12 year old son, Derry, along so he could tell me if I wasn't driving well. I phoned my old pal, Bob, who lives on the outskirts of Helena, and he agreed to meet me along the highway, wherever we found each other, and he'd drive me and Derry the rest of the way to the hospital. Years later, as Lisa and I got divorced, I looked back at her refusal to take me to the hospital as a signal moment in the process of losing track of each other in which I missed the smoke signals.

My friend Bob met us at the top of the continental divide. Derry and I got in his Audi S6, and he drove about 100 MPH the last 20 or so miles to the hospital on the east side of Helena.

I walked into St. Peter's Hospital, trying clumsily to hold my son's hand. My hands and face were contorted from hyperventilating with the pain and I hoped he didn't see my facial expressions, which I couldn't control. Bob solicitously kept a hand on my back.

We were met at the door by a starchy nurse in a blue cardigan sweater, a person of average build, and, as it turned out, of troubled temperament. I told her that I was an EMT, and that the pain in my upper right quadrant was causing me to hyperventilate. I had monitored my pulse on the drive into town and I told her it was running steadily at 80 beats per minute. I also told her that I was uninsured, and that I didn't want to pay for a lot of defensive medicine. I wasn't sure what that meant, but I hoped she'd understand. She looked at me as though I was covered with spiders and she walked over and opened the wide door to an examination room and beckoned me.

I asked her to check my vital signs. The nurse, who I'll call nurse A, told me she would decide what course the treatment for my "sore tummy" would take and to get out of all my clothes and into a gown. She closed the door of the exam room. I donned the gown, a garment designed more for her access than my modesty, and I pushed the button that summoned her back.

I was lying on the exam table with no covering but the gown, my skinny, pallid legs sticking out towards the ER admitting lobby, in plain view of anyone passing by the four-foot-wide door which nurse A had left open when she came back in. I don't know why, but it is nearly impossible for most people to pass a hospital room door without a sidelong, remorseless ogle. I asked her to close the door and to give me a paper sack to breath into to bring my hyperventilation under control. She gave me the bag, telling me that I really didn't need it. Perhaps that was why the sack was the only article from the ER treatment that never appeared on my itemized bill. She left the door open to go get a pulse-measuring device.

Besides not wanting my son to see me in these straits, I hated the fact that any of the half dozen strangers loitering in the lobby could peer up my skirt, so to speak. When nurse A came back in I asked her again to shut the door. She ignored my request while she clipped the pulse machine onto my finger and fussed with some paperwork. I nodded at the door and the lobby and again asked her to close the door. Nothing.

Finally: "Close that goddamn door."

"What ever happened to respect?" she hissed.

"What ever happened to compassion," I croaked.

As a volunteer EMT I always felt emotionally unequal to the horrifying task of extracting and "packaging" people with multiple, serious traumas who had wrecked their cars, usually drunks in the icy ditches at two in the morning. But I always tried to be nonjudgmental, to be compassionate in my every comment and movement and to reassure people that I cared about them in their predicament, and that I wanted a good outcome of our strange meeting.

Nurse A, I decided, had the compassion of a cactus. She finally spread a flannel blanket over my naked legs and begrudgingly closed the door far enough to obscure the view of me from the lobby. I had transgressed, perhaps, by showing up and using my beginner's knowledge of how I thought I should be examined. The epithet that finally led to a measure of privacy was unfortunate, but it slipped from between teeth clenched in pain, and the unsettling entry I'd made into a world that could just sweep me away.

No one in an E.R. wants to be there. They are invariably frightened and helpless, and as such, victims. Perhaps nurse A resented the fact that even though contorted with pain, I presumed to know what I wanted to happen. Perhaps, after years of treating frightened, compliant lumps, she was taken aback by my wish to participate. I had inconvenienced her routine.

At any rate, the doctor who treated me was remarkable for his quiet, albeit impersonal, efficiency. The person who drew my blood did so nearly painlessly. Finally, after two unsuccessful attempts and a parody of rusty needle revenge, nurse A got an I.V. stabbed in and started and the Demerol dripped until it masked the pain.

After three hours, and incurring $1,777.96 worth of ER, lab, pharmacy, and radiology charges I was told to see a doctor who would know what to do, and released with a prescription for pain killers.

Next day I went in for a sonogram, a $275.65 procedure that takes approximately five minutes. The middle-aged man who smeared the warm gel and rubbed the metallic instrument on my abdomen was quiet and gentle. During the exam I asked him how much the machine costs that he uses, "Quarter million," he said. I asked him how long he had been doing this work. "Nineteen years," he replied. "Do I have gallstones?" I asked. "Yep," he said.

Later that day, a radiologist with an address out near the airport industrial park, whom I never met, mailed me a bill for $150.25 for looking at the sonogram film and confirming the technician's observation.

The money was bad enough, but the interaction with nurse A and the door is what did it for me. I decided that whether intentional or not, the whole experience conspired to make me a victim, a role that I cannot accept. I resolved to do something about making the rest of this ordeal less galling, as we say.

With the gallstones confirmed, it was time to meet Doctor Dale J., who is said to be a "good gall bladder man." He entered his exam room in a flurry, a tan, youthful fifty-something man with hairy forearms and a good grip. He introduced himself almost shyly, our handshake spanned the width of the tiny examination room. As J examined me he gave me a variation on the this won't hurt much routine. I explained that what hurt worst was my uninsured status, and that I wanted to trim expenses any way possible. He said that it might be possible to leave the hospital the day of the surgery and save some money. Then we got down to the gall bladder itself.

The gall bladder is a sack that could hold two golf balls, that stores the bile your liver secretes. When fatty food drops into your stomach it is stimulated to squirt that bile. Remove it, and the bile drips steadily. Post-surgery patients report no ill effects in its absence. It is thought to be vestigial, as unnecessary as an appendix, or adenoids.

Historically, and in literature and idiom, the gall bladder is a reviled organ. Gall is synonymous with impudence and effrontery. Galls on horses are sores or tender spots caused by chafing. Bile contributes to biliousness which is blamed for bad temper, not unlike that which nurse A and I experienced.

If, in the act of gutting an animal, you pierce the gall bladder, bile spills dramatically, going right to work, digesting every surface it touches, befouling the meat, and generally raising a stink. That gall bladders are reviled, however, is cultural. In Asia, black bear gall bladders are prized for what is believed to be their power as an aphrodisiac. One time I was helping a cousin gut a black bear, a creature that when skinned, looks eerily human. A black bear's internal organs are comparable and proportionate to our human ones. In Asia, black bear gall bladders fetch more than $10,000. My cousin was very careful to remove the bear's gall bladder intact and to tie it off at both ends. He thought he might find a way to sell it in South Korea, where his brother was in the Air Force.

I asked the doctor how he intended to remove mine.

Dr. J explained that he'd make four tiny holes through which he'd stick a fiber optic camera, and some other tools and an air hose to inflate my gut to give him room to operate. He said that he'd take the gall bladder out in sections, through one of the holes.

"That won't do," I said. "Couldn't you make one incision big enough to take it out whole?" I explained: "It's worth a fortune in South Korea. I know some guys who know some guys who export black bear gall bladders, they look remarkably like ours." I thought we could pass it off as the real deal, I explained, and I was half serious.

Dr. J, to his credit, cracked a smile, and laughed. It was then that I knew I could breach the patient-practitioner wall and really talk to him. I asked him how much he'd charge for this hour-long surgery.

"Two-thousand dollars," he said.

"How do you justify that much money for an hour's work?" I asked.

"That's what the insurance companies will pay me," he said, plain as can be.

"If I pay you cash the day I get your bill, will you take a thousand bucks?" I asked.

"Twelve hundred and you have a deal," J replied and brightened a bit. "At least you want to pay. All these people who don't — their bills get spread out to all of you who do, and don't have insurance." He halfheartedly added some stuff about all his employees and the snazzy office he has to maintain, a rehashed monologue that fell flat.

Then he told me about some other things we could do to keep the expenses down. He seemed genuinely interested in doing what he could. He suggested using non-disposable instruments that he felt would save hundreds of dollars, although they take longer to use, he said, and he'd have to think about their lower cost versus more time in the operating room. He didn't seem the least bit affronted by my horse-trading, rather, he wanted to see how we could work this out. It was, I could tell, a new experience for him.

We agreed that I'd have the surgery in four weeks, an arrangement that J didn't endorse, but I was about to begin one of those rare assignments a free-lancer writer gets for which I was going to earn more than $8,000 for two week's work. J gave me a prescription for some powerful painkillers, and repeated his misgivings about waiting so long for the surgery. "Don't let the pain get ahead of you," he warned me. "Don't drive on this stuff."

His ingenuousness encouraged me to talk to the others who would be involved. When I got back from a ten-day research trip, I sent a fax to the hospital president mentioning my deal with Dr. J and asking for a meeting to discuss how I'd pay the bills. I got a call the next day from David, the hospital's vice president. We agreed to meet and I asked him to blackout the names on a couple of recent gall bladder surgeries, so that we could see what I was up against.

David, smiling, fit, mid-forties, offered me a cup of coffee in his windowless office and we looked at three bills from recent patients. He called them "customers," which sounded good, I couldn't imagine anyone treating a customer the way old nurse A had treated me.

The itemized bill made very little sense to either of us. I told David that I hoped we could find things we could eliminate; "redundant, or defensive medicine," I said, still not sure what I meant. David said, "I'm not a clinician. Neither are you. I don't see what we can do." But as we scanned the bill he wondered how much per minute the operating room costs. With his shirt-pocket calculator we figured out that along with the door charge of $420.00, the operating room charges toll at $12.50 per minute. "That might be an area you could talk to Dr. J. about," David said hopefully. I tried my cash and carry gambit, proposing to pay the day I got the bill, for a 25 percent reduction in the total. "I have a responsibility to keep this hospital going. St. Peter's is a non-profit organization, you know." He thought for a moment. "You bring your bill to me the day you get it, I'll multiply it by 75 percent and we'll save everyone some money."

I told David that I should try to talk to the anesthesia people about cutting down costs. He thought that was a good idea and escorted me to the surgical floor and right into the little office where Dr. C. and his colleagues spend their time between "cases." David introduced me.

Dr. C. is a soft-spoken gentleman, a wiry road-racing bicyclist who does more than one hundred miles on a good day. I opened the conversation asking him if he knew how much the operating room costs per minute. He didn't want to guess. When I showed him a bill he said: "That's criminal ... all the time we spend waiting for surgeons." Dr. C. assured me that he'd keep everything as efficient as he could and that Dr. J was one of the best surgeons with whom he works. He said that he'd knock me out before we went in, after the surgeon arrived, and he'd wheel me back out with alacrity.

I asked him if we could do something creative about drugs, like using generics, I suggested, knowing this ploy from conventional pharmacy wisdom.

On the recent bill for laproscopic gall bladder removal we noticed that the anonymous patient had received $905.00 worth of pharmaceuticals. This didn't include the anesthesiologist's bill, just the drugs used for a one-hour surgery. Again Dr. C. was incredulous, he apparently had never seen a bill for his work. Something called vercoronium, for instance, cost $244.00. We went down the list and he noted quite a few substitutions he could make for what he thought would be substantial savings. I asked him, however, not to skimp on the "knockouts," and painkillers. He laughed and told me he thought I'd appreciate the stuff he would use for pain.

I then phoned Dr. J and told him what had transpired, and that his willingness to deal directly with me on this expensive deal had emboldened me to talk to the others who would care for me. He agreed that we would not need another urinalysis, and that we could eliminate the $554.00 worth of x-rays that the previous patient had, although there was one that would determine whether or not any of the gallstones could have slipped down where they could do more damage, that he would use if he thought there was even a chance that I needed it. He agreed that I didn't need a pathologist, for $70, to identify the gall bladder itself, unless there was anything suspicious-looking about it. He said that there was really no need for the lab to repeat the blood work they had done just a few weeks before, although, he warned me, those numbers can change in a day. Basically, he said, he wouldn't do anything that would compromise my health.

He didn't. The surgery took 41 minutes. Eight hours later, after numerous blood pressure checks by compassionate, if bustling nurses, and visits from Dr. J and Dr. C, during which I was aware that they were evaluating me closely, I was the first patient the post-op nurses knew of who had left the hospital the same day. I gratefully accepted the wheelchair ride to the front door and saved $403.00 for going home to sleep.

Here's a quick and dirty comparison on what I saved, for the asking, over the bill for the same surgery that patient X's insurance paid:

Pharmacy	Patient X: $905.84	Me: $339.50
Med/Sur Supplies	Patient X: $1,955.23	Me: $762.25
OR Time	Patient X: $1,287.50	Me: $994.00
X-Ray	Patient X: $546.65	Me: $0.00

These figures don't include doctor's, anesthesiologist's, or radiologist's fees. From what I have seen of bills for gall bladder removals, the costs can easily run to $10,000.00. Mine cost $5,300.00 including that inspiring night in the emergency room with nurse A. No one compromised my health, if anything, they were more attentive than I knew how to ask them to be.

I went into this deal feeling as though it could have been adversarial, or that, not having medical insurance, I would be perceived as amoral or a deadbeat. But everyone negotiated with dignity. Maybe this could only have happened in a small town where much of what people do goes un-or-under-compensated, but once in a while folks hear each other's concerns and work together to be cool. Maybe this essay raises unreal possibilities out there.

A few weeks after I wrote this, my cousin Vern, the most compassionate human I know, a balding, fifty-year-old family doctor in Vancouver, read it and said he'd submit it to a periodical he received. A little while later, Dr. S., from Seattle, phoned to ask if he could publish it in the King County Medical Society bulletin, of which he was the managing editor.

"I'd be delighted," I told him. "What's your budget for a feature?" I asked, getting to the awkward part.

"I don't pay writers," Dr. S said, rather unapologetically.

"Glad to donate it, doctor," I decided.

My Dog Frank and My Cat Chuck

(previously published in *New Montana Writing*, edited by Rick Newby, 2003)

Author Note: Just another cat and dog memoir.

It's two-hundred paces from our house to our greenhouse, up a gently sloping lane under a canopy of interlaced cottonwoods and bull pines. On the edge of the slope of the greenhouse lawn resides a carved redwood grave marker with a gothic peak that faces the greenhouse. The bucolic memorial leans a bit backward, gravity has pulled it slightly downhill and it acquires a grizzled beard by summer's end from birds that alight and then void their bowels as they take off downslope. As winter progresses, the salt and pepper beard that has formed on Frank's headstone erodes with the cycles of snow and thaw. When the migratory birds return the beard grows again.

The grave marker reads:

Frank

1973-1980

Mordere Equus

Caput Demitere

Feigning sophistication for people who remark on Frank's resting place, I explain that the Latin inscription is in the ablative absolute case and reads: "To Bite Horse is To Lose Head." I think I'm right about that. More than a dozen creatures are interred in unmarked graves under the greenhouse lawn. Most of them died when the weather was unremittingly cold and that south-sloping lawn always freezes last and thaws first, so it's the place to bury our winter-killed animals. Frank got his skull caved in by one of my draft horses while they were feeding one winter afternoon. I found him inert in the corral. The horses had lipped up the scattered hay to within about two-feet of his expired body. He looked too small, but dropping dead in mud and grass hay leavings from a hoof blow to the head somehow suited him.

I have lost track of the number of times that I've arranged cats, dogs, foals, birds, fish and gerbils in the fetal position at the bottom of a hole in the terrace of cobbled river rock and clay earth that I dig out for a grave. I bury the wee creatures and sometimes shed a few tears with my kids at memories of what all we'd been to each other. Every pet is a broken heart until you end up with the ones that will outlive you. There comes a point where I must tamp the backfill into the loamy little hole and I always remove my boots and socks and pack it down barefoot.

My cat Chuck is buried out there alongside Frank, who was responsible for Chuck entering my life in a sort of perverse deal between me and a veterinarian.

Frank was an Australian Shepherd/Blue Heeler cross. He was athletic and compulsive and needed to be worked. I got him from my pal, Kim, a toothless 30-year-old gay sheepherder-turned nurses' aid who worked adroitly with Frank's mom and dad, Leonardo and Mona. Frank's parents worked with Kim at a Missoula rest home, intuitively minding the Alzheimer's patients. Sheep dogs are born to herd and are crazy to do so. Most breeds, true to their manipulated genes, want only to do their thing, so to speak. Greyhounds, bird dogs, terriers: think of it. Frank's ancestors were high bred herders and heelers and he was predisposed, it turns out, fatally, as his epitaph attests, to nip at heels and to make other animals change their behavior. All I had for Frank to work with, unlike his endlessly engaged parents, were vapid farm critters, slow to respond to fear or desire. Frank prevailed.

While I was away in the woods every day, according to Maya, my rather indignant, occasional housekeeper, Frank herded goats away from sheep and then mixed them up and started over again. He'd herd the chickens according to color, then regroup them and sort them by size. He didn't chase cats; he herded them up the lone coastal oak in the side yard.

Frank was a black and tan wee whirlwind with a heart-shaped blaze on his chest, a yellowish eye and a Caribbean blue eye that enjoyed a life of its own. He was canny and tireless, and Maya was exasperated. I knew he was wearing everybody out all day when I came home to paltry pickings in the poultry house and weary nannies with swollen udders up on my woodshed roof giving Frank the greasy eyeball and bleating goat curses.

I was horse logging, and of course the horses laid their ears back and kept him in their sights whenever he approached. But I started taking him to work with me on days that I wasn't skidding logs with the team. He loved riding in my 1949 International two-ton; the passenger's side windshield was missing. On fair days he'd creep out on the hood and position himself ornamentally. The rust and dirt coating on the rattle-canned red nose of the venerable truck gave him purchase, and I cruised at speeds that let his nose have its way as we tooled up soft, summer logging roads that I had pioneered last spring with my team.

On those days that I left the team behind and tipped trees for the horses to skid later, I'd bring Frank along. Frank started heeling the toppling trees, biting off flakes of bark as they fell. I was thinning a thick stand of fat, second growth saw logs and those creekside firs and hillside pines fell slowly as they worked their way down through the neighboring trees in a crescendo of popping limbs and wind. Frank seemed aware of the increasing speed as the trees fell, and I wasn't that worried about him. Cross-species hubris, sure, but I self-referentially empathized with him.

Some mornings, just to get the adrenaline pumping, I'd get a tree tipping; my chainsaw spitting chips from the back cut in its bole, and as it began its ineluctable descent, I'd leave my saw idling in the back cut and jump in front of it with my hands chest high and a shoulder pressed into the abrasive bark, as though I was trying to arrest its fall. Then I'd jump aside and back pedal as a ton of tree slammed to the ground and I'd feel the will to do this deal: tip a bunch of trees and then bring my horses to that logging show to skid them down to a roadside landing.

Most loggers are said to be addicted to their own adrenaline. Watching Frank harrying falling trees and then scramble clear and safe was like bonus adrenaline for me.

But Frank began to get more aggressive, taking that last-second escape farther than I ever did. Sometimes he'd jump on a tree as it was still twisting and descending through the limbs of the trees along its hammer stroke. As sunlight flooded through the lengthening rent in the canopy, Frank would scramble onto the falling tree, barking at it beneath his feet. This timber was averaging two-foot diameter butts and Frank, all claws and flexible canniness, could ride their slow wooden sine waves as the trunks bounced and levered over other logs. Sometimes, during the tree rodeo, a bouncing tree butt would launch him unpredictably, but he always got clear.

One afternoon, after a steadily intensifying day of herding trees, Frank stood directly under a big pine, yapping up at it and tearing out chips of scaly bark as his hind legs gave way to the descending weight. A couple of tons of tree trunk was going to crush him this time, but the little stud held his ground. It went too far. I kicked him out from under the bull pine just as it began pressing him to the duff.

I caught him with my steel-toed boot towards the top of his left foreleg and we both heard my boot break his humerus just as the thud of the pine butt shook the ground. He let out a surprised howl, an acknowledgement of phenomenal pain for him, and he went limp from shock. I didn't have to palpate the fracture. It swelled like a new joint just below his shoulder.

Frank licked his foreleg tentatively and yipped. I carried him to the truck, lurching oafishly over rocks and slash. I couldn't take my eyes off the swelling that grew with every step. He snarled at my clumsiest stumbles. I cradled his head in my lap as I drove the half hour down into Deer Lodge and the vet's office.

Doc Clancy was a self-indulgent old Irish lush. He preferred working on livestock, conveying condescendingly, around dog and cat people, that leaning towards the large animal practice was manlier.

He looked at Frank's leg, said it was an unusual break, and asked how it happened.

"Kicked," I coughed.

"Huh?" he said, looking up at me.

"I kicked him," I said.

His oily straw cowboy hat rose up like a stretching armadillo as he silently appraised me. Then he left the exam room. I thought: "a lecture?... the cops?... the animal authorities?"

I ruffled Frank's ears and picked sticky bark chips out of the short silkies under his chin, and Clancy walked back in through the swinging door with a writhing grain sack that he held well away from his body.

"You want a cat?" he asked.

"I'm a vegetarian," I lied.

Clancy slumped a bit but held the sack farther away from his pear-shaped torso that strained at the mother-of-plastic snaps on his plaid cowboy shirt. He eyed me with an ingenuous desperation that got the best of me.

"Well, sure, doc," I stammered. Recovering a bit, I added, "Mice. You know."

While he set Frank's leg in a cast that we hoped would prove tongue and tooth proof I held the grain sack at arm's length. It was lighter than a handful of beans and emitted tiny yowls, but the creature working to break out of the bag felt like it was kicking field goals in there. I straight-armed the sack out to the truck, wishing I had some twine to tie it shut. I folded it over on itself and stuffed the fold into the joint of the seat.

"Safe home," Clancy said, affecting an Irish accent. He laid Frank out next to me rather abruptly from the passenger-side running board, and added, "Keep the sack."

Before I even got out on the road that kitten, a bobtailed Manx, maybe ten weeks old, with a stubby tail, long, ungainly back legs, and faint tiger striping, blew up out of that sack, jumped up on the dashboard, and could have proceeded through the missing windshield and right out onto the hood, but he spied Frank. He thickened his silhouette, arched his back and bouffanted his frizzy hair. He spat towards me, like a head fake, and then leaped onto Frank's muzzle. Thankfully, Frank was still sedated. The kitten got ahold of Frank by the ears with his fore feet and milk teeth and he raked his nose a few times with his angular back legs. I grabbed the loose skin on his neck and swung him onto the seatback behind me where he prowled back and forth huffing grouchy murmurs down at the welts of blood on Frank's muzzle.

Every cat I'd ever been around was a self-absorbed nonentity, easily dismissed, but this one had my attention. He ended up standing in my lap with his forefeet on the side window frame watching for anything that moved. Sheep, cows, horses, it didn't matter, he was as absorbed as any predator.

Back home I carried my flaccid dog into the house, inspecting his traumatized face. He flopped his head drunkenly, as though to lick his broken leg, wiping hideous smears of fresh muzzle gore across the white cast. By the time I came back for the cat he was murderously eyeing the chickens from the hood of my truck. I, too, looked at those chickens as little more than food and felt an odd kinship with this powerful kitten and carried him into my house.

There was a pane broken out of the living room window that seemed to let out as many flies as it let in, that I hadn't bothered to reglaze, and I defenestrated him that evening when he peed on the mud-hued rug in the parlor. Seconds later he scratched his way back up the cedar siding, popped his head through the sharp-edged fracture in the window glass, two-stepped down the wall, walked up to my feet, and sprung into my lap. He went from purring to slobbering as I petted him. I was reading Ken Kesey's *Sometimes a Great Notion*. "Stamper" came to mind, and so he was named.

The next day, when I got home from work, I changed his name to Chuck, like the cheap steak. I had unloaded the team, slid their salty oxblood harnesses off their flanks, brushed and curried them and grained the two of them in their separate stalls. I was looking forward to frying a chuck steak that I'd left to thaw on the kitchen counter. When I walked into the kitchen the misnomered kitten was sprawled on the drain board too swelled up in the belly to jump down. He'd spent the day eating my chuck steak, six ounces of which were clearly visible in his distended gut. I reached for him and he growled protectively over the remaining scraps. Gingerly, I plucked him by the scruff and in four strides had him out the door, across the porch and down two steps, where Frank crouched avidly at my feet, perhaps realizing that this was his chance to maul the little reprobate.

I cast about to rid myself of the eponymous Chuck. In my angst and immediate need to teach him a lesson I tossed him up at the telephone line in a reaction that surprised me except that I didn't want to just to feed the defenseless little glutton to Frank. Chuck spied the black and silver wires as he ascended alongside them, and when he came back down he snagged the phone line with both fore feet and hung there, ten feet off the ground, claws sunk in plastic-coated metal wires, bawling at his fate. Chuck's softball-sized gut bobbed grotesquely as the wire swayed. His tiger stripes blurred as he kicked, trying to swing his hind claws past his bloated belly and into something. I ran back into the kitchen, grabbed a chair, and hustled back out and set the chair in the thatched grass under him. I stood uncertainly on it and tried to pull him down off the wire, which, now, he didn't want to release. Then, with the feet-first urgency of a falling cat he twisted down and sunk his claws and teeth into my forearm as the chair toppled. Aversion training, I thought, as the sod rushed up at us, can hardly be carried too far with this cat. But I twisted and took the fall on my back.

Every time I caught Chuck on the kitchen counters I'd pursue him relentlessly, grab him, whisk him out the door and toss him up toward the telephone line, which, like a port in a storm, he'd reach for desperately and then ruefully realize that he wasn't much better off. I'd hustle inside, grab a kitchen chair to stand on, and retrieve him. I got better at the chair part, and Chuck got better at sinking tooth and claw into my arm. Throughout my fifteen years with Chuck he continuously disfigured me, inflicting festering scratches and bite marks on my hands, arms, chest, shoulders, neck, and lap.

After just a couple of weeks of the high-wire aversion therapy, however, he quit pillaging my kitchen counters and began augmenting his dry food diet with increasingly ambitious and successful hunting forays for fresh blood in the grass and weeds around the house and barnyard.

One morning I walked into the barn to grain the horses and harness them prior to loading them in the truck for the short ride to my logging show. I poked my finger through the hole on the grain bin lid, lifted, and fished down in there for the coffee can I used to measure out grain portions. My hand bumped something that didn't belong in there. Before I could look or react, I felt a powerful pressure and sharp pain. I backed away from the source of the pain. As my hand emerged from the bin the pain became livelier. To this day, I admire the jaw pressure that rats can exert. This rat was shaking my middle finger, undulating his whole body as he attempted tear off an edible-sized portion. His mottled pink tail lashed my bare forearm and wrapped around it as he got all his claws buried in my skin. Utterly revulsed, I plunged my arm and the rat back in the grain bin, whipping it like I'd immersed it in acid. I lowered the lid. He let go with his snaky tail. He clawed thin air as he reached out for a better hold. His incisors gnawed away at my birdie finger. I pulled my arm purposefully out of the bin, through the dark gap under the lid. The rat let go when he figured out that my next move would be to squash his head. He'd chewed right through to the pulp under my fingernail, I noticed, as the random curses I'd been shrieking settled into self-pitying invective.

Regardless of the horses, I entertained thoughts of getting my twelve gauge and just blowing the shit out of the grain bin. Then little Chuck strutted into the barn. Most cats would flee such ructions, but not Chuck; he always checked out what might be in it for him when some sort of attractive trauma was occurring. He was about eight months old, quite a bit bigger than the rat. I baited him up to me with my bloody finger and sensibly, I reasoned, lifted the grain bin lid about a hand span, tossed him in, and dropped the lid.

Chuck's hissing and spitting muted, then I heard a muffled growl in there, then the scuffle in the shifting oats got louder, bodies thumped against the plywood walls. I harbored unworthy misgivings about Chuck's valor. Then I became compelled with the variety of squeals and screams a rat in a wooden box issues over the course of a minute or so as it is fighting, losing a fight, and dying. When I lifted the lid, Chuck was straddling the limp rat. He shot a glance up at me, growled, and went back to making a bloody mess on the rolled oats. I just left the lid open.

After winning the great coming-of-age-grain-bin fight, Chuck would take on anything, anytime, anywhere. He went after fleeing rabbits in the pasture, with his long back legs pushing him as hard and fast as the rabbit. He'd either drag them down with a forepaw or tackle them by the neck, digging in with tooth and claw like one of those educational channel lions. I'd see Chuck and a rabbit bounce up out of the bunch grass, joined in a flailing fur ball, and they'd skid to a stop together in a compact cloud of dust and dandelion fluff. Almost daily, he'd strut into the barnyard, head and stubby tail high, carrying a dead gopher or wood rat carcass or a rabbit big enough that its feet drug in the manure. He'd lie around feeding on his prey's hindquarters and eyeballing the numbskull dog, who sidled closer, absorbed by the waft of fresh meat. But Frank was never stupid enough to do any rabbit poaching. Even as the old killer slept with his prey, Frank would not tempt his fate.

Chuck became such an unrepentant hardass with dogs that I began to suspect that Doc Clancy gave me that cat to insure his own job security.

I had a large porch overlooking the county road, where I often entertained pals from the logging and ranching communities. Someone had added an old school bus seat to my couch and an overstuffed chair and my porch was a gathering place for an eclectic group of workers in the extractive industries who convened for card games, conviviality, cold beers from the aluminum cooler, and quiet talk as we composed ourselves after our various days' exertions. My guests often had dogs with them. Any dog with the temerity to swagger onto our porch or make some sort of nuisance of himself while Chuck lounged on the railing ended up at Clancy's animal clinic.

Using the move he'd put on Frank on his ride home from the vet's, he'd leap directly at the dog's head, the dog would duck reflexively, whereupon Chuck would dig his teeth and front claws into the dog's head, neck, and ears while the claws at the ends of his long back legs slashed repeatedly into nasal passages that burst into gore and improbable canine keening.

Chuck became adept at riding noisy dog heads around the porch. Although he never got as good as, say, a professional bull rider, and rode for an honest eight seconds, he began going longer and longer, sometimes pausing in the muzzle shredding to regain his balance, and then raking vigorously again with both hind legs. I believe he began experimenting with driving and steering the dogs. The whole deal would last a few seconds, then Chuck would bound across the dog's back and settle back onto the porch rail to regard what he had wrought: a stunned dog owner cradling a bloodied muzzle in his lap, and the beer swilling jades who'd seen all this before, who tacitly admired Chuck's swift and sure enforcement of porch decorum.

At the risk of reverse anthropomorphization, I feel that Chuck had intuited a sense of propriety from me and the lads. Loggers generally seek low-toned small talk after a week of moving huge weights around with a modicum of control. Those of us who had survived that business for a few years regarded longevity as a matter of pure chance. We didn't test our luck getting wound up and acting loud and bulletproof during our leisure time. At least the crowd that passed the jug and joint on my porch didn't. Somnolent dogs raising their noses into breezes never provoked Chuck. It was those feckless dipshits who disturbed the serenity of the porch that got the nose job.

I kept a few of Clancy's business cards handy and gave the victims' owners directions to the clinic. I always offered to pay for the doctoring if it ever happened again. No dog ever stepped on the porch unbidden after encountering Chuck. After a few years of the same friends and their dogs coming over, there would always be a dolorous pack of cow dogs and curs watching Chuck from the yard. They looked related, with their matching, livid scars running down their muzzles, like a pack of mutant baboons. To his credit, Chuck allowed the deferential hounds under the porch roof. They had to keep their tails down and appear to placate him.

Chuck, in his dotage, slowed down as did I, fathering two kids as heedfully as I knew how. Hunting, I presumed, became less rewarding for Chuck as the risks increased. But he'd still disappear for days. I don't remember the last time I saw him alive in the spring of 1990. The daughter of one of my old cronies found him submerged in our creek in what became a poignant vignette at one of our Mother's Day Maypole parties when three wide-eyed kids alerted me to Chuck's demise in Warm Springs creek. They watched me kneel and stroke Chuck's body under six inches of water. More kids showed up, murmuring to one another.

I don't know why, maybe because a bunch of kids were watching, wondering if they should be horrified. I unbuttoned my shirt and lifted Chuck's dripping, limp cadaver out of the water and tucked him next to my skin. I walked up to the greenhouse lawn with him in my shirt and dug his little grave with a rock pick and garden trowel and a coterie of solemn kids watching and I told them the story about Chuck and the grain-bin rat. I took him out of my shirt and curled him up at the bottom of the hole and salty tears disappeared into the freshwater that slicked his striped old hide. Then I scooped dirt onto him by hand, took off my shoes and socks and tamped the backfill barefooted.

There are so many critters buried under the greenhouse lawn that I hesitate to dig there anymore for fear of exhuming a skeleton. But I know exactly where Chuck is buried, next to Frank, near that gothic marker with the Latin inscription in the ablative absolute case.

A Sled, a Cow, the Future

(previously published in Mountain Gazette, Winter, 2007)

Author Note: I wrote this to memorialize my decision to sell the place I built from scratch, where we raised our family. I lived at and built the Harpfarm from 1977 through 2014.

Few people may believe that at age 57 I recently T-boned, so to speak, a pregnant, thousand-pound cow while riding my Flexible Flyer sled down the steepest county road in western Montana. To rural sledders this is plausible, but perhaps not to adults of my generation. The mean age for the 55,000 sledders injured badly enough every winter to need an ER visit is 9.9, a dismal statistic that reveals a paucity of baby boomers still willing to have fun hurtling down mountains with a modicum of control. Sledding down icy back roads is a pure and noble calling which offers countless opportunities for high speed rides on metal-runnered sleds that are somewhat steerable. Obstacles to doing so abound, from so-called common sense, to cows, like the one I collided with a while ago. Thanks to a triad of medical miracles: Advil, Irish whiskey, and denial, I am fully ambulatory; no longer limited to looking at the world over my left shoulder. So, facing the old computer screen head on, here come the facts.

Before the belaboring the embarrassing facts, however, let's dispense with a possible sidetrack. I was not "cow-tipping," that is, engaged in the quasi-athletic, nocturnal activity in which alcohol emboldened ruralites and frat rats—an often overlapping demographic - putatively try to topple cows who are believed to be asleep on their feet. Cow tipping is probably little more than an urban myth because cows, as stupid as they appear, disturb easily, and it would take at least five drunks, as stupid as they appear, in a coordinated, stealthy effort to accomplish an actual cow tipping. Cows seem to daydream much of their lives, but they sleep lying down, and warily. They awaken with alacrity and could easily avoid a group of humans deranged enough to aspire to "tip" them. Drunken ruralites would more likely turn their attentions to sheep, whether they are sleeping or not, but this is an essay meant for families, not those of you prurient enough to hope I am pursuing the more aberrant avenues of animal husbandry. On the topic of sledding under or into cows I shall layout the simple truth, for once. That's what participatory journalists who dabble in gravity sports and incur head injuries vaingloriously attempt to do.

Harpole road, the county road that accesses my place two miles northeast of the Montana town of Avon, has for 30 years presented me with the best sledding that I will ever know, even though at times I'm forced to share that road with cows. Every few winters conditions conspire to offer optimal sledding; we get around eight inches of snow, then it thaws briefly for an afternoon which causes some surface snow to turn to water that percolates down through the underlying snow crystals. Then, with sundown, everything refreezes and the overlying snow acquires a denser crystalline structure while a layer of pure ice forms on the road surface. When these conditions occur, each time I drive back and forth over the mile-long hill into my place, I purposefully groom the road for sledding. I make increasingly wider sets of tire tracks, packing the snow into "runs." I'm the only one who uses Harpole Road in the winter so I call the county road crew and ask them to not plow the road as I prepare it for sledding.

Despite numerous mishaps, I remain an inveterate adrenaline addict, and gravity, snow, and ice have played into that jones all my life. In December of 2006 the optimal freeze/thaw cycles occurred daily, a very weird weather pattern that we never saw much before the 90's, and a repeated pattern that I've adapted to. Daily thaws and nighttime refreezing make good ice and great sledding, but that's a troubling, relatively recent winter weather pattern I've managed to take advantage of.

After about a week of fastidious grooming, both sides of the mile-long hill on Harpole Road were pure, gorgeous snow-packed ice all the way, the fastest conditions I'd ever seen, and this was just the middle of December. A few dozen of my neighbor's cows were grazing the edges of the road and pastures on the east side of the hill resulting in some cow turds on the two tracks I'd been grooming, but I always hope to drive over them and flatten them before they freeze. I often walk the road and hockey-stick loose turds off it. I resist the urge to flat-out kick the turds that I haven't flattened or scattered with my tires before they freeze. When the excreta hits the snow it is the temperature of the inner cow and easily, organically, melts down to bond with the road surface. Warm fodder resides there and melts the snow that cradles it as it seeks its origins and then the cow's outpourings transmogrify into ice reinforced with chewed grass, a mass that hardens immutably. I have seen heavy steel snowplows mounted on eight-ton trucks bounce off those glacial turds like a Zamboni happening upon a speed bump. As for the cows themselves, I figured that if I had to, I would be able steer around them.

My hubris and one misbegotten cow resulted in another wreck to rack up in the uncountable, perhaps incomprehensible total of sledding mishaps I've weathered, as we say, during this 50-year avocation. I decided to delude myself that I'd be going past them so low and sizzling fast, that they'd never process the fact that I was there until I was past them. And besides, they spend very little time on the road itself, since there's no grass on it. I was on the slippery slope of denial that seduces all adrenaline addicts. But before this account starts moving too fast, a little background:

I've had a long, glorious, at times, egregious, history with Flexible Flyers, those low sleds with the slatted wooden decks, red metal runners, and the curvy steering cross which you grab when prone, or push with your feet when sitting. My first sledding wreck put me in the hospital, in 1962, for three months while a doctor named Cedarblade repaired a broken femur and attempted multiple skin grafts to repair an avulsion of skin and muscle on my right leg where it was nearly torn off. My parents and eight siblings and I had just arrived at a mountain park west of Denver with a steep slope blanketed in crusty snow. I pulled a rusted old Flyer from the back of the '58 Chevy station wagon and in a move I'd premeditated to avoid sharing a ride with a sibling I held the sled to my chest and sprinted down the hill and belly flopped the sled onto the hardpan snow and gained momentum and reached a hellbent speed faster than I could figure out how to control my trajectory.

The absolute beauty, the transcendent fineness of these wild junctures where you give yourself over to gravity is that they put you entirely in the moment. I held no regrets about my eight siblings up there behind me, nor did a speck of apprehension for the future cloud my thoughts. Sledding focuses one completely on what's right there in front of you, even if you don't know what to do about what you see coming. With legs flailing, toes digging at the crust, I was attempting to brake or steer. As I gained speed I pretty much gave up on gaining control. Then I came to a patch of rocks that stuck out of the snow a couple feet and a knifey granitic intrusive that was pointed uphill intruded through my jeans and into my right leg where it was hanging over the edge of the sled. I felt immediately like I had seriously skinned my knee, but I had flayed my entire right thigh as my momentum halted. I rolled off the sled and beheld a flap of skin twice the size of my hand hanging diagonally across my knee and lying flaccidly down my shin like an extra-large slice of pizza. Torn grayish muscles and my jagged pinkish femur were as plain to see as a poorly butchered flank steak lying in my lap. I didn't believe that this apparition could be my leg, then I couldn't stand up and then I didn't believe that I would live through this trauma and I said a good Act of Contrition, as the nuns had taught me because I knew this was God's punishment for masturbating.

It took a year and six surgeries to get back to where I could walk. It was another year before I could play basketball.

I have never since headed prone on a Flexible Flyer down an unsurveyed hill, and I usually choose to sled down roads. A smooth sluice of pure ice on a road is way faster and safer, in some ways, than an unknown mountainside. Hence my grooming of Harpole road when conditions are incrementally adding up to better and better sledding. It is as though the weather wishes to lead me astray by degrees. Although my aptness for conducting myself beyond the pale is a fact.

During the twelve years that I was an avid skydiver, in several hundred free-falls I experienced terminal velocity, in which the weight of my body falling through the sky equaled the air pressure pushing at me. When you can't fall any faster you are at terminal velocity. Sailboats have a terminal velocity called hull speed, at which they can't slice through the water any faster. Most objects have a speed that they can't exceed. Theoretically, sleds do not have a terminal velocity, except that you eventually run out of hill to slide down because there's a constant vector of downhill energy adding to your velocity while you are being sucked down a hill by gravity. Extreme skiers, even with the coefficient of friction that occurs between their skis and the mountain, have been clocked at higher velocities than free-falling skydivers, because the slope of the mountain is always adding to the impetus of gravity, giving you the cold shoulder faster and faster. The promise of a mountain pushing you down itself, whatever your conveyance, is nearly as beguiling as what you learn about yourself when stepping out of an airplane into the sky: it is the promise that you are gaining self-knowledge in an extreme situation. Gravity sports heedfully pursued are exercises in character building.

So here I was of a Sunday afternoon in the diffuse daylight, where the horizon and white-blanketed earth made a dreamy ambiance, like playing inside a glass of milk. The world was monochrome, the horizon was indistinguishable. Bleached grey fence posts and inky barbwire defined the landscapes, even the cows were black angus. The most vivid visuals were my dogs blurring around. My current pack of mutts elicit superlatives, they are, respectively, the dumbest, wildest, and homeliest I've ever had. Max, the eldest, was supposed to be a miniature Australian shepherd but his recessive genes went recessive and he ended up the size of a normal Aussie. He's liver and white with one Caribbean blue eye that enjoys a life of its own, but his brain must be smaller than one of his eyes. Big Fawn looks like a Labrador with tiger stripes; she's a pit bull/St. Bernard cross who I rescued from a trailer full of meth chefs near Anaconda. I believe she was tweaking involuntarily as she was weaned and she remains about half feral. My son, Derry, named her Fawn and, ironically, they became her favorite dish. Every dog you get dies and breaks your heart until you end up with the one that outlives you. Wee Ernie, when I drove away from the dog pound with him, struck me as the one that'll outlive me. He's a wiener dog/Scotty cross who is the color of bleached straw and about five times longer than he is tall. He'd been adopted and returned to the animal shelter four times in his first year because he is an escape artist. Since there's no place to escape to from where I live, my nearest neighbor is three miles away, Ernie entertains himself catching pan-sized brookies from the creek. Ernie goes fishing alone. Sometimes he goes fawning with Fawn.

On the first walk up the east side of the hill the Flexible Flyer offered practically no resistance, sliding along behind me at the end of a macramé of ropes and lanyards that had been added to it by my kids over the years as they attempted to harness various family dogs. As I looked over my shoulder at the sled my gaze rested upon the location in the Garnet range foothills where I'd built a place from scratch since 1977. Lisa and I had raised our family there for 20 years, then the empty nest gave us no good reason to stay married. It looked to me now like a ghost town, and I felt estranged from my own history out on this hill. A graybeard unswayed by conventions, ready to sled. Ask any mid-fifties guy, he probably feels like he's as ready as he was at thirty. I surely missed my kids and I loved my dogs for all their observant companionship they unwittingly provide. As I ascended the two-track I counted seven frozen cow turds randomly spaced down the quarter mile run on the left track of the road, but dozens on the right, fleetingly evoking rural Montana politics.

A couple dozen cows in their sixth month of gestating what looks like Subaru's in their distended undersides silently grazed, their big, black heads pendulously sweeping snow aside to get at the grass. Every year they spend a few days between the fences, grazing the "long acres" alongside the edges of the county road before they head down to the riverside meadows where they are fed grass hay through the winter. I like that they graze down the roadside flora because eating all those grass and clover stems helps keep the snow from drifting later in the winter. The cows along Harpole road hardly lift their heads when I drive by them, they are treated gently. In their world they ask only for grass, water, and sky and probably they equate vehicles with food; quality of life, like a lot of us.

Before setting out on a sledding day I claw around the soap dishes and put a few of those lenticular remnants in my chest pockets and use them to lubricate the runners before each trip down. The steam emanating from the unzipped top of my coveralls can fog my glasses but it smells slightly of Irish Spring, an oddly comforting aroma on a cold hillside. I am not, however, blaming the wreck on fogged glasses.

Fawn, and Ernie, both in their first winter with me, curiously watched me prepare for what was to come. They sensed my friskiness as I lay on my sled and began kind of breast stroking downhill to get started. But the pups started yipping and dashing in at me, playfully, to be sure, but I was afraid they'd end up with a leg under the runner and my 175 pounds on top of everything, and we'd be headed to the veterinarian.

My dogs must think their first name is "godamit," at times because that is a special word I save for occasions when I want them to change their behavior immediately. With one magic word, delivered righteously, prefixing their names, I can stop them in their tracks. Then they were out of sight because I was racing down that hill faster than they could run, something like 25 MPH.

Dodging the cow turds down the left track added an engaging slalom for the Flexible Flyer; there was a kind of rhythmic flow to the ride. My face was about a foot above the road and the wind chill and speed caused tears to flow back into my ears. Over-steering slightly edged me into the slower, less packed road's edge or center and bled off speed heartbreakingly. I eschewed sitting because going prone feels about twice as fast with my face inches off the surface, and the lower profile is surely slicker and swifter.

Every runner sled has a point, whether you sit or go prone, where you can feel the right amount of weight on the forward part of the runners that allows for optimal steering while minimizing the runner friction. Truthfully, the phrase "optimal steering" and the word "sled" don't belong in the same sentence, but as you naturally go for more speed, you must kid yourself into believing that things are under control. On my second run I reminded myself that just like turning skis, one also should throw a little weight on the runner opposite the direction you wish to turn. I was hurtling down the ice more efficiently on each run, getting smarter, going faster and faster. I was thinking, "luge" and feeling Olympian. On the trudge back up in the bracing temperatures mouthfuls of air tasted like peppermint infusions. One soon learns the rewards of the sledders' uphill trudge, a pace that allows conversation. Alone, I was singing verses of "Whatya Do With a Drunken Sailor," for which Ernie improvised, then quickly aborted a puny howl.

The east side of the hill on Harpole road slopes straight down through a pasture, a run that is a quarter-mile long and for every one hundred feet you travel you descend six, a six percent grade, where an adept sledder on ice may even exceed 25 MPH. There are no fences near the road on the downslope east side. There were a few cows grazing, but far enough away that they paid no attention to my dogs or me. My dogs were minding me and the nose worthy things they find to sniff at in the snow. They weren't making any cows move against their will. I can't blame the dogs for the wreck.

After a half dozen runs down the east side I decided to take a look at the longer, much steeper west side of the hill, where the county road snakes through two easy turns and 17 percent slopes. Consecutive unscathed runs in terrific conditions had trapped me in the deadly confluence of insouciance and impulse. I had been sledding down the slow side of the hill and believed that I was ready for the west side of Harpole hill and possibly doubling the speed I'd been enjoying. I stood at the top and looked down the narrow corridor that the fences created, maybe sixty feet wide, with its steeply sloped drop-offs on both sides. According to my GPS the road drops 165 feet in its half-mile meander down the west side of the hill, the equivalent of sledding off a 16-story building and ending up three blocks away.

When my grandfather pioneered this road into his gold mine in 1931 he simply drove right up the narrow spine of the hill which rises from the riverside pasture like the neck of a supine horse, establishing a sinuous trail up a hill over which you could hit a golf ball with a seven iron. I looked down that half-mile long hill and thought steeper is better, and I knew this would be the fastest sledding I'd ever done. I decided against walking all the way down the hill to survey the road for turds because I felt that I could dodge anything I came across. Plus, I was still catching my breath. There were a few cows grazing the edges between the fences. I couldn't see the entire length of the road because it drops so steeply in a couple sections. I stood at the top of the quarter-mile long slope and felt pleased with myself for being out there getting up a sweat on a 12-degree day, and I was sanguine about how well prepped the road was and there was a hint of Irish Spring in the frosty air. Clean fun.

I re-soaped my runners and paused and admired the view of the Little Blackfoot river valley and the peaks of the Flint Creek range some 30 miles to the west. Then I placed the Flexible Flyer on the right side track and pushed and chased it awkwardly, like a roadrunner chasing a lizard, and then I belly flopped onto it. I barked a gratuitous "godamit" over my shoulder at my dogs that I quickly outpaced. In fact, by the time I'd admonished all three dogs I was ripping down the road too wantonly to even consider arresting my trajectory or rolling off the sled.

What happened next I can only attempt to recreate. The 17 percent grade kept accelerating me, everything seemed to be happening about three times faster than my runs down the east side. The wind chill on my face stung now and I bounced over a frozen turd before I could even think about steering around it, the sled was briefly airborne and adrenaline kicked in like powerful fizz in my veins. Grimly and giddily, if that's possible, I figured that this ride would take every bit of concentration I could muster. I'd sped down more than half the hill and was still picking up speed, and I was focused on the surface just ahead, hoping to avoid frozen cow patties. My eyes teared up, seriously blurring my vision. I blinked hard and squinted, wishing I had thought of ski goggles and I knew I was moving as fast as I do on skis. I must have been doing about 40 miles per hour.

The second steep drop on the road isn't visible until you get to its crest. Just over the lip, in the middle of the road, a big mama cow faced me, her head low, she looked to have each of her legs fleeing in a different direction, she was sprawled on the ice and not going anywhere.

The only sensation from the collision was an explosion, complete with blast pressures that seemed to fill my head and reverberate into my chest. Getting knocked unconscious is really kind of prosaic in its predictability; you "see stars," as they say, and a few times when I've been knocked cold, when unconsciousness took over slower, I've gotten a lightshow replete with strobes. An unexpected sense of weight bears down precipitously somewhere on your head as you hear a loud crack and that's about it. It can happen so fast that you didn't have a chance to avoid it. Then, with the passage of time you awaken. If you don't wake up that is not getting knocked out, it's getting killed.

I guess, between my many years of horse logging and timber falling, some amateur boxing, and my predisposition for gravity sports, I've been clocked a couple dozen times. It has usually happened when I was around other people and, of course, I awaken to voices and hands on me. This time I awoke to silence. Max was sitting practically on top of me eyeing me quizzically. There are no animals that more closely observe humans than dogs. Wee Ernie was keeping his nose in the breeze a few feet away and Fawn, right next to Ernie, was watching me stir. Max has dog halitosis and I wanted to tell him, "You stink," but I couldn't speak yet. I could not figure out how I ended up ragdolled on a snowy hillside with the sunset congealing and my dogs somnolently hanging out. I never take them skiing with me. My head, left shoulder and neck felt stretched and hot. I wear a helmet when I ski, twice it has saved me from certain concussions and I wondered where my helmet was, not realizing yet that I hadn't been skiing. Although the times I've been knocked out skiing I didn't know what I'd been doing or where I was for a while either.

I assumed that I'd been unconscious for quite a while because palpating my skull I found a well-developed lump growing above my left ear. I felt my head and looked at my hand and there was nothing. I felt my ear and saw blood on my glove, but I couldn't tell if it was superficial. Sour grass-smelling cow slobber had time to freeze in my hair and beard. Then I heard a cow mooing contentedly away somewhere, like they do towards the end of the day and they've had enough to eat for a while, and I began, dimly, to piece a picture together.

I believe that blows to the head alternately knock sense into or out of you. Where I stand in that cycle is no longer apparent. I remember looking up at my dog Max's blue eye, and I reflexively daydreamed about snorkeling. But the intimate smell of fresh cow shit insinuated itself and I noticed an elongate smear across my shins. I had been out long enough for the nearby cow pies to quit steaming. I was sort of draped over some basketball-sized rocks and regaining myself and clinically curious about what price I'd pay in broken bones, torn connective tissues, and memory loss this time. If you can wiggle your toes and then lift your legs you have a lot to work with. I could, but I couldn't see anything clearly much beyond Max's eye and knew I'd lost my glasses. I saw the amorphous track I left in the crusty roadside snow where I had bounced and skidded about 20 feet off into the ditch and crawled back up onto the road. That I couldn't imagine standing up saddened me. My glasses were back up on the road, partially glazed in frozen bovine saliva and crusted over with snow, but intact, if icky. I wiped at them with a clean hankie I had tucked in my back pocket and, looking through them, I felt less disembodied.

I thought about being knocked out, lying there invisible to the world in a ditch on a late December afternoon with the temperature on its way south of zero. I felt somehow in arrears with the world, like I'd never make up the lost time. My sled was a ways down the road and bent beyond any notion of sliding it home. I crawled to it. Kneeling, I picked it up; the birdlike lightness of it seemed improbable. Crawling downhill had magnified the pain in my head, then my neck and shoulder aches coalesced and I gave out, toppled, and vomited and took solace identifying some dried blueberries I'd been snacking on, as though I was reassembling fragments of my day rather well. Back down in the snow I cupped my hands around my face and paid attention to my breathing. I was hyperventilating, curled up on the county road in my earth-toned coveralls, no more noteworthy than a cow turd.

The cows grazed phlegmatically, none of them apparently injured by the Flexible Flyer or me. I rested my head on the sled and looked straight up, the milkiness of the day was just cold now, the sky curdling towards darkness; then I thought it looked like the inside of an oyster shell, then a dirty dishrag up there, then the dull side of a piece of tin foil. Then I realized I was cycling through winter-sky clichés and that vaguely alarmed me. That I just wanted to rest up, maybe take a little nap on the road, suddenly felt like an undertow tugging at me. I mustered myself from the lethargy of trauma and stood up, using the sled like a cane. I stood still until I could pick the sled up. The walk back over the hill, trying not to jar my head, favoring a shoulder and stiff neck, carrying the sled skeleton like a broken bird under my right arm, was the loneliest I'd felt since I can't remember. I released the dogs with a whisper and they loped home well ahead of me.

I topped the hill and my place came into view, the ten buildings, the gardens and lawns and basketball court and trampoline blanketed in pinkish snow; areas I'd made unnaturally flat, if not level. The pond and folf course and swing set and tree house, and fire pit and no one to play with. I sat on my bent sled and thought about all the days I spend alone up this valley where I've lived more than half my life and made a place for my family. For three years it has just been me up here, all the good noise we raised has been sifted down to me whispering, and this day I'd come close to being a ghost, and that fact had me sobbing. Had I not come-to, there would have been no one to find me before I died of exposure while unconscious. The isolation of my place had never made me feel so vulnerable. Had I frozen to death in the ditch, melting down into the snow, no one might have found my body for days.

Then I came to a decision that made me think later that I'd just had some sense knocked into me. Soon after the kids left for college my wife and I divorced and since then I'd been living alone and I decided I should sell the whole shitaree and move closer to other humans, where someone might find me if I was about to expire in a ditch.

A couple days later I met my kids in Helena, at a craft brewery lit by loud lights with tall tables and chairs where they were hanging out with other college folks home for Christmas break. I apprised them of my decision. We had all assumed that I'd be hanging onto the place where they were born and raised and Flannery and Derry would some-day inherit it. Their faces went through shock, disbelief, confusion, and Flan burst into tears while Derry sat introspectively, not giving up much emotion yet. I cried a little. Then Flannery, with some effort, composed herself, wiped her tears away, and said, "Good, Dad, you've spent 30 years out there, building anything anyone wanted and making a living for us. Do something for yourself."

"You're amazing," Derry told his sister, and they hugged for quite a while. Then he turned to me, shrugged and smiled, and said, "You did a good job on us," and he hugged me. "Do something for yourself."

We're not done crying about turning our backs on the place yet, but that meeting made me prouder than I've ever felt about my kids. I was sure that it'd be okay to move closer to town. I told them I didn't know what to do about moving my dogs because they're about half wild. Derry said, "Dad, you're about half wild, this is going to be interesting."

I asked them if they'd have time over the Christmas break to go skiing for a couple days. We all bemoaned climate change and the way it has decimated the number of days we get to ski fresh snow, let alone, powder. If there are any archconservative climate change deniers reading this you might as well just stop reading right now, if, indeed, you can read. I deplore the shortsighted rapaciousness and disregard that humans continue to show for our world. Our emissions are bequeathing our children a battered planet that will look nothing like what we are accustomed to and there seems to be no all-embracing, no global resolution to mitigate our mutilation of the world our offspring are inheriting.

The daytime thaws and nighttime refreezing that made sledding so good is portentous, unearthly weather, a threatening pattern that Montana winters have become. But I know that if the weather presents good sledding, I'll be back at it, albeit helmeted, focused on another interlude with gravity as my Flexible Flyer delivers me into the future.

Marching in Moscow for what it's Worth

(previously published in *Crocodil,* the first free press in Russia, Winter, 1992.)

Author Note: I walked through Moscow streets with a couple of journalists during the largest protest movement in Russian history.

I rode the Moscow Metro's Koltsevaya (circular) line to the Barricadnaya station on March 28, 1991, with two Soviet friends, an interpreter and her husband, to take part in the great demonstration against Gorbachev's intention to place the Moscow Militsia under the jurisdiction of the Ministry of the Interior. My Muscovite sidekicks knew that all the Metro stations near the city center would be closed, as is the custom whenever there are large events near the Kremlin. City officials honestly fear that a crush of riders larger than the stations and platforms were designed to accommodate would result in accidents.

There are more than one hundred Moscow Metro stations, each an architectural masterpiece clad with any of fifty kinds of marble. Every station has its own motif expressed with statuary, bas-reliefs, monuments, back-lit stained glass, or tile mosaics set in ceiling cupolas depicting Russian history, heroes, industry, or generalized images of Soviet life. The colonnaded concourses are kept immaculate by fierce, bent, broom-wielding babushkas (older women who wear colorful scarves). When the trains come roaring and squealing from the tunnels into the stations, crystal chandeliers sway in the cloying sweet stink of creosote.

During World War II the Metro stations were inhabited. Boards were laid on the tracks at night for the millions of women and children and others left behind. A certain sort of society is said to have evolved in this subterranean infrastructure. These days, the raucous workaday underground delivery of people can obviate speech and riders' facial expressions go solemn, as though recalling nights spent in a bomb shelter. But the Metro is by no means devoid of enjoyment.

Pleasure in Moscow comes rarely and in small ways these days. Some commuters seem to relish standing with only the soles of their shoes in contact with the random kinetics of a hurtling train while engrossed in some reading material. Support from seats, handrails, bulkheads, or one's fellow passengers is eschewed for the mental and physical challenge of blithely perusing a newspaper or a book while remaining seemingly rooted. In a country where chic is unattainable, where personal style is impossible to actualize, poise counts. And more than any possession, knowledge confers status.

We emerged from the Barricadnaya station into the diffuse gray light of late afternoon. To our right was the zoo with its attendant redolence and the outlandish calls of caged birds. We joined the throng passing to our left, linking arms as is the warm custom of Russians. In the graceful manner of strolling Muscovites we took care not to splash one another's shoes as we encountered standing water in the innumerable potholes. This was the after-work crowd that on any other day would be packing the sidewalks and riding the Metro home. But this evening they were a walking voice from curb to curb, untroubled by traffic. Comrade Popov, the mayor of Moscow, had closed to vehicles the streets likely to be used by the marchers, an act that bestowed his imprimatur on the demonstration. As we walked down the center of Sadovya Road, my friends pointed out landmarks such as the former residence of Beria, the bloodiest of the KGB chiefs, the planetarium, and Chekhov's house.

We then approached the first ranks of the Militsia—the Moscow city police – whose very presence was at the crux of the demonstration. The Militsia had been ordered by Gorbachev's Minister of the Interior to prevent or impede the protest march. This usurping of the powers of the Moscow Soviet by the Prime Minister, in addition to the enormous presence of the Soviet army in the city center, was an unconscionable totalitarian backsliding that provoked this march, the biggest demonstration in the history of Moscow. Many marchers said they never before had seen so many uniforms in Moscow. I never had seen so many military vehicles in a city. We knew that water cannon and tear gas had been approved for use on the people. We could see that other weapons were at hand.

I found myself near the front of the marchers. The Militsia we approached were ranked four-deep, curb to curb across the streets. They were outfitted in riot gear, holding clear plastic shields and long white batons. As we neared them they were unsmiling as subway patrons, a grim wall of blue wool greatcoats. The front ranks of marchers hesitated, but only slightly; the ripples of momentum were pressing at our backs and suddenly we were within a baton-length of the Militsia. When we were but a step from them, they simply turned sideways, in concert, in much the way passengers do to expedite the ingress or egress of others on the Moscow Metro. The decorations on their epaulets and the shiny brass fittings on their coarse wool coats indicated tenure. Most of these men were experienced Moscow cops. The first two men I passed between had eyes as flat and inwardly focused as those of martyrs depicted in icons. Our eyes met but we learned nothing of each other except that they were not working for Gorbachev, and so they stood aside. They wore their acquiescence with stoic dignity. We accepted our passage in kind. We passed similarly and without fear or confrontation through the ranks of Moscow Militsia three more times along the path of the march.

The other uniformed presence was that of the soldiers who lined the sidewalks and footpaths at the edge of the streets. Thousands of puerile conscripts crowded the byways and, as ordered, did their best to provoke the marchers' anger. Their peach-fuzz imprecations focused on body fluids and functions and cast ancestral aspersions, but were wasted on a crowd forewarned and bent on larger issues. The soldiers crowded archways and portals where behind them inner courtyards partially concealed tanks and armored personnel carriers idling in clouds of ominous, gray Soviet diesel fumes.

By the time we passed the Satire Theater and the imposing columned facade of the Tchaikovsky Theater we had reached Mayakovsky Square. The provocative slurs of the young soldiers diminished, and other words spread through the mass gathering around the heroic statue of Vladimir Mayakovsky, the romantic poet of the Revolution. We heard that marching to Red Square and the Kremlin was impossible because tanks and trucks completely blocked the avenues of approach. We heard that there was a crowd of similar proportions a few blocks away at Pushkin Square, the place in Moscow for the soapbox foment and pamphleteering that is tolerated more and more these days. This wasn't a speaking rally in Mayakovsky Square, there was no bull horning. It was simply a huge assemblage of people willing by their very presence to reject unjust dicta from a government they want to trust. We had marched for perhaps an hour and stood chatting for another hour and occasional bits of news spread slowly through the crowd like breezes. Word passed that deputies in the emergency council of the Supreme Soviet had come to blows over the opposing positions that led to the gathering of this vast crowd. Finally, word spread that after a vote of the deputies, Gorbachev had failed to place the Moscow Militsia under the control of the Ministry of the Interior and that he acceded to Yeltsin's demands to remove the army troops from the city center by the following day. The news was received with quiet pride and some joking references to the tactics of fish market harridans having prevailed again in the Supreme Soviet. My friends seemed tentative, however, unwilling to ascribe the political change the demonstration wrought with any sense of celebration. They spoke of hopelessness on the horizon and problems so much bigger than those who pretend to solutions. Optimism in general in the USSR is regarded as a limited view of a complex world. Optimism precludes contemplating the whole picture. My Russian friends aren't pessimistic, but they are inured to the constant prospect of tragedy and betrayal.

Quite suddenly, after two weeks of overcast skies, the half-light of a northern latitude sunset cut under the cloud cover. Snow clumps fell in that windless square, those big doily-like configurations that you can watch dropping for seconds. The snow fell through the pinkish hues of sodium-vapor lamps and blurred the Byzantine, Italian, and modern architecture that surrounds the square the size of a futbol pitch.

As darkness congealed, this mass of convivial demonstrators chatted in groups while the snow collected on fur hats, scarves, and bare heads. A few comrades near me looked up tracking the descent of big flakes and licked them out of the lowering sky like tasting nascent democracy; perhaps but a fleeting, melting moment.

The purpose of the demonstration was served. Yeltsin, it was felt, had consolidated power and withstood a strangely out-of-character political maneuver by Gorbachev that had backfired, and the crowd began to dissolve. All the nearby Metro stations were still closed and we walked a couple of miles southwest speaking of the veiled civil war that had been waged for over seventy years by the Soviet government against the people. Had we just participated in the last skirmish? Some of the positive changes that have occurred in the Gorbachev years are that the people now understand the many ways they have been misused by their Socialist government. They feel that this is their history and heritage and that even though they have been given the right to vote, the most common needs of a decent life will always be out of reach. But my Soviet friends have voted at the polls and with their feet and hearts and they will enmass again and face young soldiers and partially concealed weapons if that is what is required to attain dignity. We had peacefully deflected what was hoped to be Gorbachev's misbegotten attempt at dictatorship. All the potential for a bloodbath was in the streets that night but the black hearted propensity for killing the masses is no longer extant in the Soviet Union.

We sought an open subway entrance, and found the first open Metro station at Park Culturi. The vaulted arches and walls throughout the station depict in carved marble bas-relief various athletes in 1930's garb and stylized Stalin-gothic poses. It was curiously sullen down there, quite crowded, and stank of wet wool. But the difference between oppressed silence and the dignity of facing a challenge patiently seemed to mitigate the quiescence.

One train on the Metro holds upwards of 700 people. Occasionally the driver, through mindlessness, carelessness, bad equipment or maybe low-down ugliness, throws the riders around abruptly and unpredictably. What distinguishes a driver as plain mean are the uneven starts, the acceleration in fits followed by spastic braking. These rides are awfully trying for the riders. People abandon their reading materials and look for handholds and support. They look sideways gauging whom they might step on and who to look out for. Their reading forgotten, they simply hang on enduring another insult and hoping that when they transfer to the next train, they will be in the hands of a decent driver.

Acknowledging Praise

At around forty years of age, after twenty years of making a living logging, the collective effects of several injuries suggested life changes. That epiphany led me back to Carroll College, in Helena, to study writing, and away to Ireland for a year of school at University College Galway, and a year in the Irish National Writer's Workshop.

Back home, I began sending my writing to national magazines. I wallpapered our two-hole outhouse with rejections from a dozen or more glossies with millions of subscribers. I also showed my early writing to an array of accomplished writers who offered didactic critiques and praise that emboldened and propelled me. I learned how dishing out praise is elemental to encouraging others whose yearnings we appreciate, to proceed with confidence. The poignancy of qualified praise; investing the praisee with particular, certain, appreciation of what all they got right, cannot be understated.

All of that is to express my profound gratitude for the teachers, editors, workshop facilitators, literary friends, translators, interpreters, and even the strangers who have taken the time to comment on my writing in letters to the editor. I tried to assemble a list of all the people I'd like to acknowledge and it ran to more than a hundred names, and I'm sure it was incomplete. So, I'd simply like to acknowledge the value of praise as we encourage one another to pursue creativity.

This eulogy has hung above my computer for thirty years and informs every go-around I get into with writers and students of writing. Roger Angell, the sublime baseball writer and essayist for the *New Yorker* wrote this upon the death, in 1992, of William Shawn, the redoubtable editor of that magazine.

"Journalists like to think of themselves as tough birds, old pros. It's a business, this writing game, and when you finish this piece it's time to go and knock off the next one. But Shawn, who was tough as manganese-molybdenum in some ways, knew better. He had somehow perceived that writers are desperately in need of praise for their work—wild for it. The hard creative process, even when it's only getting things down on paper for a magazine, isn't just another line of work, but also represents the writers' semi neurotic need to rearrange the world, to set it out in more orderly and appetizing forms. It is something a child would do, and children can never get enough praise, especially if it comes in the form and person of an adult who will give them full attention, attention beyond measure. Praise makes them grow and go on, and those who bestow it are remembered vividly, even after they are gone."

— Tom Harpole

Helena, MT

November 7, 2020

photo by Joe McBryan

In 1970, Tom (*Harp*) Harpole and his cousin Jerry put together a horse logging show in western Oregon through most of the 70's, while he studied for a Forestry Engineering MA at OSU. He got banged up falling timber in western Montana in the early 80's and he and his wife Lisa took the Work Comp settlement and headed to Ireland with their wee ones, Flannery and Derry. Harp studied Latin, Greek, and English writing and was selected to be the first American to participate in the Irish National Writer's Workshop. Two years later, back home, he began writing for a living at the age of 40 and did well, working for glossies such as National Geographic, Sports Illustrated, Smithsonian Air & Space, plus more. Magazine assignments took him to six continents over a twenty-three-year career. He also spent several hundred days, two weeks at a time, teaching writing workshops in 80+ bush schools all over Alaska.

Certain magazines that assigned Harp feature articles knew early on that he would try anything that involved physical/emotional risks. He regarded himself as a Survivor's Euphoria aficionado. His willingness and perspective on dalliances with danger range from an N.F.L. record, to horse logging, to skydiving with Russian cosmonauts, to getting a black bear stoned, to his compassion as a volunteer EMT in rural Montana, to protesting Gorbachev in 1990, to driving ice roads above the Arctic circle, and more.

For further reading of our award winning essays & poems, check out ONE-SENTENCE JOURNAL, by Chris La Tray.

"Reading Chris La Tray's One-Sentence Journal I find myself wishing all kinds of things: that I went for more walks in the woods, that I spent more time in the company of owls, that I ate more fried chicken, that I woke each day in time to watch the sunrise. For this is a sunrise book, a book of revelations, of creekwalks and roadfood and ordinary sadnesses, ordinary joys—which are, in the end, the only kind. 'I have a stake in this,' La Tray writes. And so do you. So do you."

— Joe Wilkins, author of *Fall Back Down When I Die* and *The Mountain and the Fathers*

Printed in the U.S.A.

www.riverfeetpress.com